NEW ✳ MAP
ITALY

HERBERT YPMA

NEW ✳ MAP
ITALY

UNFORGETTABLE EXPERIENCES FOR THE DISCERNING TRAVELER

500+ illustrations

Thames & Hudson

INTRODUCTION

I can't quite remember which airline started cheap flights. Was it easyJet or Ryanair? Not that it matters. The fact is they are now ubiquitous. If you've got £150 to your name, you can get a return flight to Venice, Rome, Paris, Barcelona or pretty much anywhere else in Europe.

Even if you leave it to the last minute, there are so many budget airlines that you can always find a reasonably priced flight going somewhere. And the stress that travellers would often feel when choosing somewhere to stay has been diffused by the likes of Airbnb, which already has more addresses around the globe than the world's top hotel chains put together. In fact, if you live in London it's probably cheaper to spend a weekend somewhere in Italy than it is to stay at home.

In a nutshell: there are no longer any barriers to travel.

Travel used to be for the well organized, well heeled and well connected. If you travelled, you were one of the lucky few. Simply wandering around without agenda or plan was good enough. Nowadays travel is for anyone who can navigate a website or an app. And that's good! But – and you knew there was a 'but' coming – it has put extraordinary emphasis on the age-old question: What do I do when I get there? 'Easy to get to' means having to share with everybody. When you go to Rome, Venice, Milan, Florence, Verona, Capri, Naples, Taormina or Lake Como, making spontaneous discoveries is next to impossible – they are just too crowded. As well as the crowds, you often have to contend with crafty, unscrupulous hawkers jostling to extract as much money as possible from you.

Finding the real Venice or Rome – or anywhere else for that matter – requires a new depth of knowledge. So how do you avoid the tourist traps if you're visiting somewhere for the first time? How do you find the restaurants that are popular with the locals? Or the shops that offer something different or unique that you won't get on the high street? How do you explore a place in a way that will make you remember this trip for the rest of your life?

The answer to all these questions is knowledge. Knowledge that you can trust is the key, and I'm not talking Google, Wikipedia or TripAdvisor here. If you want to discover the hidden gems – places that still hold something special – you need to consult a source that doesn't have sponsored search results or thousands of indistinguishable reviews by people you don't know.

'So why should we trust you?' I hear you say. Travelling has been in my blood since childhood, and I continue to journey all over the world as a photographer. As a result, I have published around thirty books in the fields of culture, design, architecture and travel. Italy in particular has drawn me back time and again, and I've explored just about every part of it. Some cities, such as Rome and Venice, I've visited more times than I can say. Whenever I've stayed over, looking for interesting, individual spots to photograph and write about, the owners have been kind enough to introduce me to the best restaurants, the quirkiest shops and the places most loved by the locals. This adds up to a lot of knowledge that I have never stopped to share...until now!

HOW TO USE THIS BOOK

A few years ago I was in Venice having a coffee with Gioele Romanelli, whose family own the charming Hotel Flora as well as the more exotic Hotel Novecento in Venice. He had some questions about my new book on Italy, and somehow the conversation drifted to Sicily. 'Have you finished your chapter on Sicily?' he asked, and I responded that, yes, I had.

'I would love to take my family to Sicily,' he confided. 'Can you give me any tips?'

For the next twenty minutes, I did just that. I laid out a basic itinerary of suggestions – where to go, where to stay, where to eat and what to do – in the Sicily that I know, together with a brief explanation of why I was recommending them. Enthusiastically, he took down all the information I provided, and then it was time for both of us to get back to work – he, managing his Venice hotels, and me, photographing his Fortuny-inspired Hotel Novecento.

Eighteen months later, I caught up with Gioele again in Venice, and enquired, again over coffee, whether he had managed to get to Sicily.

'We certainly did,' he replied. 'It was perfect!'

'What did you do?' I asked.

'Exactly what you suggested!' he answered matter-of-factly. 'We went to Taormina, stayed at Villa Ducale, walked down the never-ending steps to the beach at Isola Bella, took the kids to learn about ancient Greek theatre, and spent hours mesmerized by the views of the volcano and coastline. From there, we went to Monaci delle Terre Nere, in the shadow of Mount Etna. Then we moved on to Casa Talía in Modica, enjoyed our breakfast with a view, raced the kids up all the stone stairs of the town on our way to dinner in Modica Alta and drove out to the beach at Pozzallo, where the children practised rolling down the sand dunes into the turquoise sea. Finally,' he continued, 'we spent a night at Gutkowski in Syracuse and tried out Ortigia's wonderful swimming platform.'

I was astounded and deeply flattered that he had taken my advice so literally, but his feedback also proved invaluable to me because it helped to define – for me as much as the reader – what this book is about and how to use it. Is this a comprehensive book on Italy? No, I don't think so. In fact, I'm not even sure how to define 'comprehensive' when it comes to travel.

I only know this: the places in Italy that I have written about, photographed, stayed in, explored and researched and revisited numerous times, are the only places that I recommend and feature. They are what I know, what I have discovered – not via an internet search or social media consensus, but through good old-fashioned trial and error. These gems – and only these gems – are what I am sharing in this book, and they come in four different guises.

ECLECTIC EXPERIENCES

Taking the night boat from Naples, jumping off the cliffs south of Otranto, jumping on an elegant water taxi in Venice, cycling along the Arno, swimming the walls of Dionysius, exploring the forgotten farmland of Sicily's interior, combining the beach with the baroque, finding the best *gelati* in Rome... There are more than twenty eclectic experiences documented in this book. And you don't need to be Bear Grylls to embark on any of these adventures. The only thing you need is the time and the desire. The rest is easy.

STAYING IN CHARACTER

Borrowing a phrase from the thespian world, the thirty-five places to stay featured in this book range from the grand or eccentric to the small and quirky, but what they have in common is that they all embody the soul and character of their location and setting. Culturally, aesthetically and emotionally, they are in step with where they are. Whether it's sleeping next to a sloshing canal in Venice, dozing under the rumbling plume of Etna's active volcano, enduring a monastic silent dinner in Umbria, living in a 'four star' cave in Matera, sharing a Puglian farmhouse with animals, or waking up to a view from Homer's *Odyssey*, 'Staying in Character' means creating memorable experiences effortlessly...simply by staying overnight. Surely that's the whole point of travel?

CONVINCING CONTEXT

Sometimes a little bit of history goes a long way. The uniqueness of hiking to the ruins of Tiberius' villa on Capri, for instance, is definitely enhanced by some background on this Roman emperor. Similarly, ordering a cappuccino in the café that used to be Canova's studio, on Rome's Via del Babuino, surrounded by magnificent plaster maquettes of his work, is more meaningful if you know just how famous Canova was in his day. Throughout the book, relevant nuggets of history are introduced with the simple and sole purpose of enhancing the experience.

LEGEND FOR LUNCH

We all want a memorable place to have lunch, don't we? It doesn't have to be fancy or expensive, just consistently good and soulfully memorable – worthy of at least one dinner-party conversation back home. And it should be in keeping with the destination. In other words: not a Thai restaurant on an Italian beach. There are eight such legends featured in this book. That's not a lot, granted, but legends are few and far between.

SICILY

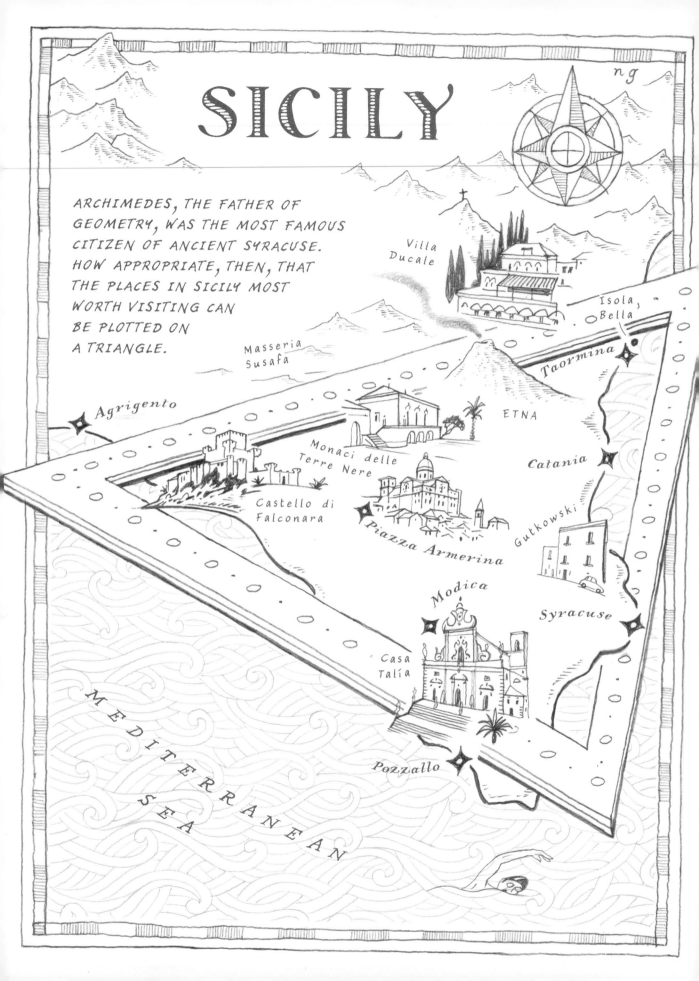

The Clue
to Everything

*To have seen Italy without having
seen Sicily is not to have seen Italy at all,
for Sicily is the clue to everything.*

Goethe, *Italian Journey 1786–1788*

Sicily is special for many reasons, from its pale beaches and turquoise waters to its forgotten farmland and the imposing presence of Etna, Europe's largest active volcano; from the early Greek refinement of places such as Taormina and Ortigia to the splendour and extravagance of the Sicilian baroque. Together they make a powerful, lasting impression. Fly to Catania and take a week to work your way around my map by car and you'll discover a world that will stimulate your mind, your soul and your tastebuds, as well as doing wonders for your suntan.

For centuries the empires of the Mediterranean fought over Sicily, the most coveted prize of the ancient world. Phoenicians, Greeks, Carthaginians, Romans and Moors all plotted and schemed to own this, the largest island in the Mediterranean. The appeal was simple: Sicily was not only rich, but it also had the best location strategically. As invaders took turns in conquering and colonizing the island, each left its mark – helping to shape a culture that has made Sicily one of the most diverse and cosmopolitan spots in the Mediterranean. No other place in Europe can offer such an exotic blend of architecture and art. Factor in the island's culinary wealth, spectacular geography, and abundance of sea and sun, and it's no wonder that so many airlines are now flying directly to Catania and Palermo.

THE MOST BEAUTIFUL BAROQUE

In 1693 a devastating earthquake ripped through the east coast of Sicily, destroying most of the buildings and killing more than 60,000 people. Rebuilding started almost immediately, with great flair and embellishment, in a style that eventually became known as Sicilian baroque. Architects from Sicily, many having trained in Rome, were commissioned by the Catholic Church and by Sicilian nobility to construct new cathedrals, churches and palazzi in the style of the time – and the style of the time was baroque, a fancy word for 'fancy'. To this highly extravagant style, characterized by ornate detail, they applied even more embellishment, with grotesque and comical faces carved in stone known as *mascheroni* and a preponderance of *putti*, the chubby little angels that adorn these elaborate buildings.

It's fascinating to contemplate the wealth that made all of this construction possible. Sicily, at the time, was rich. It was one of the most successful agricultural exporters in Europe. The lemons for which Sicily is famed were in high demand due to the growing taste for lemonade, which would become an 18th-century obsession. Even more lucrative was Sicily's dominance in the wheat trade. Sicilian durum wheat was much sought after, even more than Sicilian wines, lemons and olive oil. The source of the island's wealth was the produce of the land, and the land, without exception, was owned by the aristocracy.

During the baroque period, there were essentially two kinds of people in Sicily: the *paesano* (peasant) and the *nobile* (aristocrat). In the 1600s, Sicily's feudal system counted some 87 princes, 36 counts and over 200 barons. The Spanish ruled Sicily via a viceroy and, following the establishment of the infamous Spanish Inquisition in the late 15th century, Sicilian royalty was afraid of only one thing: the Church. So they gave – and they gave generously – which is why a town like Modica was able to build a hundred churches in a style and manner that towns in other parts of Italy could scarce have afforded for just one building.

In addition to their patronage of the Church, the *nobili* also gave generously to themselves in the form of grand houses. All landed families had a palazzo on their vast farms, but life 'at court' meant they also needed a townhouse – preferably in both Catania and Palermo because the viceroy divided his time between the two cities. As a result, the aristocracy spent less and less time on their estates, neglecting the management of their farms and their *noblesse oblige*, the unwritten obligation to protect their workers. Continual absence not only watered down the yield of their estates, but also created an opportunity for criminals to thrive by offering the

protection (at a price) that the nobles were supposed to provide. These are the origins of Sicily's notorious Mafia – a term that derives from a Sicilian word meaning 'swagger' or 'bravado', describing the boldness of this underbelly. The decadence of Sicilian aristocracy was beautifully documented in the novel *Il Gattopardo* (*The Leopard*) by Giuseppe Tomasi di Lampedusa (himself a minor prince), published in 1958 and later brought to the silver screen by Luchino Visconti in a film starring Burt Lancaster, Alain Delon and Claudia Cardinale.

However, it wasn't just the self-indulgent extravagance of the aristocracy that would ultimately bring an end to the wealth: it was, bizarrely, the American West. Who could ever have imagined that the prairies of Kansas, Nebraska, Oklahoma, Colorado and Texas would dominate wheat production from the early 1900s onwards to such an extent that the world wheat price would halve almost overnight, and never recover? Yet that's exactly what did happen. Today Sicily has a sad magnificence about it. The wealth has disappeared, along with most of the princes, counts and barons, but the legacy of their building spree has survived.

So, as you climb the countless steps from Modica Bassa (Lower Modica) to Modica Alta (Upper Modica), and you pass the myriad townhouses with ornate terraces and *mascheroni* carved into the stone beams that hold them up, or as you marvel at the quantity of intricate detail in the churches that stand on every other corner, try to imagine just how many lemons and how much wheat had to be cultivated to pay for it all.

CASA TALÍA

A Panorama of Modica's Baroque Treasures

Modica, with its abundance of churches and elaborate ornament, is Sicily at its most exotic. The old town is like a monumental tableau of uniformly coloured, artfully carved stonework, squeezed onto the steep face of a canyon and connected by countless flights of steps. Navigate with Google and you quickly learn that most 'streets' are actually staircases. It is a charismatic place, exquisitely preserved, and from a distance – from the other side of the canyon that divides Modica in two – it enthrals you with an unbridled panorama of the divine excess of Sicilian baroque.

Modica's compelling beauty – together with Sicily's laid-back way of life – is what inspired Viviana Haddad and Marco Giunta, two architects from Milan, to seek a slower pace. They chose to raise their family here, and they committed to building Talía as a place that would offer visitors the best experience of Modica. 'Talía' means 'look' or 'admire' in the Sicilian dialect, which is the perfect name for this beautifully designed compound. Its ten rooms, two houses and spectacular garden are all about the views. To put it simply, Talía has the best views in town.

The rooms are set in meticulously renovated cottages facing the old town, and Viviana and Marco have made the most of being on the 'wrong' side of the canyon. There are no churches or fancy townhouses on this side, only workers' cottages built in a simple, rustic style – a style that the architects have embraced wholeheartedly. Working with an authentic menu of stone walls, lime plaster, cane ceilings and floors laid with traditional tiles, they have created an attractive and honest series of spaces that are reassuringly comfortable, yet also strikingly contemporary. The plates, the glasses, the cutlery, the furniture and even the food are as attractive, modern and original as they can be. Each room is unique, but they are all united by one thing: the owners' distinctive style, a perfect blend of tradition and modernity as seen through the architect's eye.

COMBINE BAROQUE WITH THE BEACH

After two days of climbing Modica's many steps (and there are a lot of them!) and photographing *mascheroni*, and *putti*, heroic statues of saints and elaborate details of doors, lintels and recesses – in short, all the ingredients of Sicilian baroque – I'd had enough. I needed a break. So I asked Viviana, the owner of Casa Talía, what she does when she wants to get away from everything baroque.

'I take my kids to the beach,' Viviana told me.

'What beach?' I shot back. 'We're in a canyon, in the middle of the countryside.'

'Yes,' she replied, 'it's deceptive, but I promise you there's a beautiful sandy beach fifteen minutes from here.'

I didn't really believe her but I wanted to, so I gladly took her scribbled instructions and drove out

of town in my rented Panda. After four wrong turns that only took me deeper into the countryside, eventually I ended up at the beach at Pozzallo – the one she takes her kids to. It was better than she had described: broad and sandy with dunes and proper waves, and there was no one there. It was the kind of beach you see in travel brochures and wonder where it is. So now you know: it is fifteen minutes from Modica.

Discovering this beach changed my perspective of Modica. 'Beach plus baroque' is much more interesting than baroque alone, and much more in keeping with my search for *la dolce vita*, 'the sweet life'. It helped me craft the perfect Modica day, and it goes something like this. Start with breakfast in Casa Talía's garden: deli-

cious organic food, freshly squeezed orange juice and *that view* – the sweeping panorama of old Modica. Then, it's an action-packed morning exploring the extravagant excesses of Sicilian baroque. For which your reward will be lunch in Modica Bassa, at Osteria dei Sapori Perduti on Corso Umberto I, followed by a lazy afternoon of swimming, sleeping and sunning on that beautiful beach that no one knows about at Pozzallo. Then, in the evening, make sure you're back just before sunset for an *aperitivo* at Talía, once more making the most of that view, before you brave the steps again for dinner in Modica Alta, in the splendid and stylish Locanda del Colonnello on Vico Biscari. This is the proper way to 'go baroque' (sorry, I couldn't resist!).

SYRACUSE

Sicily's Melting Pot

More than any other Sicilian city, Syracuse showcases the full spectrum of Sicily's unique heritage: ancient Greek ruins, Roman amphitheatres, baroque cathedrals, Norman forts, neoclassical palaces and narrow medieval laneways woven together in a historical tapestry that easily justifies the town's Unesco World Heritage listing. Add to this the fact that the old town, Ortigia, is now packed with cute cafés, great bars and funky little authentic restaurants, and you can understand why it has become one of Sicily's most dynamic attractions.

If you want a break from all the history and heritage, you might like to know there is a white, sandy beach – Fontane Bianche – only fifteen minutes out of town. Or you could go to Lido di Noto, about thirty-five minutes away, and combine a swim with an excursion to the town of Noto, stopping off for a coffee at its famous Caffè Sicilia (Corso Vittorio Emanuele). If you go further still, there's the tiny fishing village of Marzamemi, known for its authentic charm and fresh fish: eat at La Cialoma (Piazza Regina Margherita) after a swim at Calamosche beach.

Dionysius I was the ruler of Syracuse, one of the most powerful city-states in the ancient Mediterranean world. Originally founded as a Corinthian colony, it prospered due to its unique location.

BUILT BY DIONYSIUS, THE FORMIDABLE 10-METRE-HIGH SEA WALL THAT SURROUNDS THIS ANCIENT TOWN OFFERS ONE OF THE MOST ORIGINAL EXPERIENCES: TO SWIM ALONG ITS EDGE. AS YOU LEAVE THE WATER AND

A winged Pegasus and the Corinthian helmet appeared on ancient coins of this city-state.

CLIMB ONE OF THE IRON LADDERS FIXED AT INTERVALS ALONG THE VERTICAL EXPANSE OF STONE, YOU HAVE AN INKLING OF THE EXCITEMENT THAT BREACHING A CITY WALL MUST HAVE BROUGHT IN ITS DAY.

GUTKOWSKI

Converted Warehouse on Ortigia's Waterfront

When I first visited Ortigia in 2001, Gutkowski was a small boutique hotel with seven rooms in a newly renovated building. I was there to meet Paola Pretsch – an architect with a Polish grandmother – who grew up there and knows the island like the back of her hand. She was the first to make the brave decision to invest in a boutique hotel on Lungomare di Levante, a street that runs along the top of the old sea wall, in a city that was, at the time, in a state of semi-ruin.

Ortigia was halfway through a monumental restoration funded by a grant from the European Union. Sensing an imminent change, and an opportunity, Paola purchased a small warehouse on the eastern seaboard of the island. It was not in the most elegant part of town, but it did have the immense 'plus' of being right on the waterfront. It was small and simple but also refined and beautiful, with a pared-down design aesthetic that was rare in Sicily in those days. I loved it, and I loved Ortigia, even though half the town was still under reconstruction. The next time I visited, fifteen years later, Gutkowski had expanded to thirty rooms, with the addition of a second, much larger waterfront building and an acclaimed restaurant serving 'neo-Sicilian' cuisine, called Gut. Paola was there to greet me again, and apart from the nostalgia of seeing each other after a decade and a half she was pleased to report that being in my *Hip Hotels Italy* book had put Gutkowski on the map, so to speak. Both Gutkowski and Ortigia had changed for the better. The island is full of interesting bars and great restaurants, as well as Sicilian baroque gems such as Syracuse Cathedral, officially the Cattedrale Metropolitana della Natività di Maria Santissima, which basks in the splendour of its newly completed restoration. This extraordinary church has some incredible features, including the surviving Doric columns of the Temple of Athena, built in the 5th century BC, which have been incorporated into both the façade and the interior.

ENGAGE WITH AN ACTIVE VOLCANO

Mount Etna, rising majestically behind the city of Catania on the east coast of Sicily, is not only the tallest volcano in Europe (3,329 m), but also the most active; so active, in fact, that it is erupting almost continually. The argument is that this rumbling makes the giant safer because the constant eruptions act like a safety valve, reducing the possibility of an eruption on the scale that buried Herculaneum and Pompeii. Nevertheless, Etna has had its share of spectacular moments. Virgil dedicated a poem to one of her eruptions, and an earlier explosion in 396 BC was of such fiery magnitude that it is said to have scared the Carthaginians, who had arrived to lay siege to Syracuse, all the way back to Carthage.

Yet, considering the long history that Sicily and Etna have shared, not many instances have resulted in loss of life, and so Sicilians continue to live in her snow-capped shadow and farm her rich volcanic soil. In the winter, people from nearby Catania even brave the slopes of her peak to ski at a small resort that doubles as a refuge. In the same way that Mount Fuji is indelibly associated with Japan, Etna is an unmistakable icon of Sicily.

MONACI DELLE TERRE NERE

Sleeping in the Shadow of Mount Etna

In the 18th century, Franciscan monks from the Order of St Anne came here – to the rich volcanic slopes of Etna – to work the land. With sweat and toil they built terraces of black lava stone overlooking the Mediterranean below, in order to cultivate vineyards and make wine. They also built a road in black stone, the same road that leads to the property today. When this order of Franciscan monks died out, for centuries the carefully constructed terraces were left unattended. That is, until Sicilian-born Guido Coffa found the abandoned vineyard one day when he was riding past on his scooter.

What Guido had stumbled across was a 24-hectare farm with a dilapidated 19th-century house and a series of cottages in total disrepair. Despite the state of ruin, he decided, then and there, to dedicate his life to farming. The plan was simple: rebuild the terrace walls, replant vines, renovate the main house and fix up the cottages. The list of things to do was very long, but remarkably Guido did them all and more. Perhaps you can put this down to the fact that he was trained as an engineer, but I think there's more to it than that. The reason Monaci delle Terre Nere (which means 'Monks of the Black Earth') is such a success is because Guido's focus is on the agriculture. Monaci makes its own wine

from grapes grown on its restored terraces. It also grows its own organic produce that is served in its celebrated restaurant, Locanda Nerello.

But I doubt that guests see Monaci as a place of advanced agricultural practices. What they see is an amazing place to stay that serves delicious organic food and obscurely wonderful Etna wines. At the risk of stating the obvious, Monaci delle Terre Nere is not your typical *agriturismo* experience. Technically, yes, you are the guest of a farmer, but this farmer is as serious about design as he is about agriculture. The converted lava stone cottages that serve as accommodation are charismatically authentic and rustic on the outside, and as contemporary as it gets on the inside. In all, Monaci has twenty rooms, some of which are located in the main house.

Monaci is the kind of place you are reluctant to leave, even for the day. And why would you? Everything you could want from an Etna experience is here: sweeping views, historic vineyards, authentic architecture, and a fuming volcano breathing down on your organic breakfast in the garden. For Guido, the black earth is Mother Earth. It is what he knows, what he grew up with, and the embodiment of his dream. As he so poetically puts it, 'Monaci embraces Etna... and Etna embraces Monaci.'

TAORMINA

The Setting that Seduced the Intellectual Elite

Almost floating above the blue Mediterranean like a cloud, with the snow-capped peak of Etna fuming in the background, Taormina has been celebrated for its views for millennia. There aren't many places on the planet that can compete with this ancient corner of Sicily for sheer spectacle and beauty. Goethe, Guy de Maupassant, Oscar Wilde, Tennessee Williams, Brahms, Wagner, Nietzsche, Jean Cocteau, Truman Capote and others spent time here, and many writers produced some of their best work installed in hotels and villas framed by the unique panorama of volcano and coast. Goethe wrote a travel book called *Italian Journey* here; Nietzsche wrote *Thus Spoke Zarathustra*; Nobel Prize-winning Icelandic author Halldór Laxness wrote the first of his modern novels, *The Great Weaver from Kashmir*, first published in 1927; and D. H. Lawrence, in residence at Villa Fontana Vecchia between 1920 and 1922, wrote a travel book called *Sea and Sardinia*. More scandalously, it was rumoured that *Lady Chatterley's Lover*, which Lawrence also began while living in Taormina, was a disguised tale of his wife's dalliances with a Sicilian mule driver.

Ever since settlers from Magna Graecia first built a splendid outdoor theatre here high above the sea, framing Mount Etna like a monumental painting, Taormina has been a geographic 'muse' to artists and the arts. These days, however, it can seem more circus than muse. There are just too many tourists for such a small town, and on some days there are so many people milling around that you almost have to get in line to turn a corner. Yet it is still possible to find *la dolce vita* in Taormina. You just have to rise above it. Literally!

On the road leading out of town, there's a seemingly endless set of stairs chiselled into the mountainside that winds its way up to a tiny chapel, Madonna della Rocca, perched at the very top. If you climb all the way up, you will be rewarded with a view few people see. The crinkly coastline, far below, spreads out in front of you as if you are looking at a map, and Etna provides such a perfect backdrop that you can see why, in the late 1800s, the first people invited to view Baron Otto Geleng's paintings of Taormina at a gallery in Berlin doubted if any of this was real. So frustrated was the German artist by critics' continued scepticism that he issued a bold challenge. 'Come to Sicily,' he proclaimed, 'and if Taormina differs from my paintings, I will pay for your journey and accommodation; otherwise you will write of its beauty in your newspaper.' And write they did.

UP AND DOWN TO ISOLA BELLA

Taormina is a gem – a crowded gem. The solution to selfishly enjoying the spectacular beauty of this unique combination of volcano and coast is to stay high and go low: venture above Taormina to avoid the crowds and then head down to Isola Bella for a swim. The view from Taormina is a panorama that no mortal will tire of, and the higher you go, the better it gets. Plus, once you get above Taormina, you leave the tourist flock behind.

Villa Ducale is the perfect place to make the most of this legendary destination. Situated far above Taormina, with a spectacular view of the Bay of Giardini Naxos and the snow-capped

peak of Etna in the distance, it is one of those places we secretly hope to find and pledge never to tell anyone about. It's a magical place to have lunch, and an even better place to stay. The view is omnipresent – from the terraces and balconies of the guest rooms, from the restaurant, and even from the stairs leading down to reception.

While the views speak for themselves, what may not come across so readily is the warmth with which guests are treated at Villa Ducale. You are hosted by a very well-connected local family led by the energetic Rosaria Quartucci. Most of what I know about Taormina, I learned from her. She is the one who showed me the steps that lead down to town – it takes just ten minutes to walk down them, but half an hour to climb back up – and the secret spot behind the church of Madonna della Rocca that has a view of the bay framed by a stone garden gate.

She also took me to Hallington Siculo, a beautiful public garden that few visitors seem to find. Hidden in plain sight in the centre of Taormina, the garden was created by the English eccentric Florence Trevelyan as a tribute to her native country and donated to the town following her death. Born into an aristocratic family, Trevelyan made Taormina her home in the late 19th century and is buried near Castelmola, above the town.

A talented gardener and a pioneering conservationist (of birds, in particular), Trevelyan also bought the Isola Bella and set about establishing a garden with native Mediterranean and exotic plants. This picturesque gem, flanked by steep cliffs and surrounded by turquoise waters, is now a protected sanctuary and popular beach destination. Her Taormina was the Taormina that inspired many famous writers, and she fought to keep it that way. On her death, her precious isle was left to her husband, and subsequently to members of the Trevelyan family; in 1990 it was bought by the regional government of Sicily and is now run by the Italian arm of the World Wide Fund for Nature, securing Trevelyan's legacy for future generations.

VILLA DUCALE, TAORMINA

Truman Capote

Nietzsche

Halldór Laxness,
*The Great Weaver
from Kashmir*

Jean Cocteau

TAORMINA IS BOTH MUSE AND MASTERPIECE.
NOWHERE ELSE IN THE WORLD OFFERS A VIEW
LIKE THIS! THE EXTRAORDINARY COMBINATION

Tennessee Williams

Guy de Maupassant

D. H. Lawrence,
Lady Chatterley's Lover

Oscar Wilde

OF VOLCANO AND COAST - SEEN FROM AN 'EAGLE'S
NEST' PERSPECTIVE - HAS INSPIRED COUNTLESS
WRITERS, POETS AND ARTISTS SINCE ANCIENT TIMES.

Goethe, *Italian
Journey 1786–1788*

THE THEATRE OF ANCIENT GREECE

The Origins of Modern-day Entertainment

Tragedy, comedy and satire were invented by the ancient Greeks as dramatic genres to aid their esteemed and beloved art of storytelling in theatre. They valued the spoken word over the written word because it could be adapted and interpreted, and as such it was admired not only for its content, but also for its dynamism. Nearly all forms of drama that we enjoy today, from opera to cinema, stem from ancient Greek theatre. That's why Taormina's gem is so important: it is a remarkably intact souvenir from the ancient Mediterranean world and it is also – as Goethe wrote of Sicily as a whole – 'the clue to everything'.

Thespis (6th century BC), for example, who is said to have been the first actor in Greek theatre, is the origin of the alternative English term for an actor, 'thespian'. At the time, plays were performed on a round, flat area known as the orchestra, which was normally situated at the bottom of a hill; the hillside provided the viewing area, known as the *theatron* (literally 'a seeing place'). The word 'scene' derives from a structure directly behind the stage, the *skene* ('tent'), through which actors could enter and exit the performance. Even the expression *Deus ex machina* ('god from the machine'), describing an unexpected power or event saving a seemingly hopeless situation, stems from the Greek word *mekhane* – a crane used to lift actors, particularly those playing gods, into the air to give the impression of flight.

So when you visit Taormina's splendid Greek theatre, the second largest in Sicily, it is worth bearing in mind that you are not just stomping around a relic: you are standing in the middle of the very place that launched the entertainment-hungry culture we live in today.

EXPLORE SICILY'S FORGOTTEN FARMLAND

My favourite scenes from *The Godfather* are when Michael Corleone is sent to Sicily, to stay in hiding after a particularly bloody inter-family feud in New York leaves Don Corleone's family vulnerable to retribution. The landscape of the favourite son's exile is the straw-coloured, sun-bleached farmland of Sicily's interior. It is ancient, beautiful and majestic, and every hilltop seems to host a village more quaint and charming than the next. It is here that Michael Corleone discovers the simple life – an agrarian existence dictated by the seasons, by the heat and the sun, and by the harvest from the rolling fields stretching into the distance. It's not surprising that he falls in love here, and his marriage – with the men dressed in snappy black suits and white shirts (and leather-strapped shotguns casually slung over their shoulders), dancing with striking beauties on stone-paved courtyards – conjures up the epic charm of Sicily's forgotten farmland.

Sicily's interior, the land that separates Catania on the east coast and Palermo in the northwest, is mountainous and rugged in parts and rolling and cultivated in others. It has a timeless quality: age-old villages perched on peaks stand guard over the fertile valleys below, connected by an ancient network of winding roads. The countryside is magnificent and empty, reminiscent of New Zealand or Patagonia in its remote beauty. While it's not uncommon on the roads to be brought to a standstill by a shepherd crossing with his goats, you might never meet another car. Most surprising is the weather. In some places it can be quite cold. For instance, in Polizzi Generosa – birthplace of Domenico Dolce, one half of Dolce & Gabbana – it snows in the winter. Even in summer, when the rest of Sicily is baking in the Mediterranean sun, the mountains are still surprisingly cool, especially at night.

MASSERIA SUSAFA

A Monumental Farm Straight out of The Leopard

It wasn't long ago that hundreds of people depended on this farm. Situated 1,000 m above sea level, not far from the town of Polizzi Generosa, Masseria Susafa is massive – the kind of farm that made Sicily rich. One glance at the grain store, which is the size of a small cathedral, tells you this was the backbone of Sicily's thriving agricultural economy.

Owned by the Saeli-Rizzuto family – as it has been for more than a century – Masseria Susafa is still a farm, and farming remains the main source of income. But for the sake of efficiency and modernity, the actual farming equipment – the massive harvesters that now do what once would have required a small army of workers – is housed in a more up-to-date complex in the next valley, hidden behind a nearby peak. Which poses the question of what to do with all the old buildings?

It was Manfredi Rizzuto Saeli who came up with the solution, transforming Masseria's old farm buildings into a guest experience. And experience is the right word. Just getting here is an adventure. At Masseria the first thing they will ask you is how you intend to travel. If you are renting a car, then they will 'strongly' suggest you get a Panda – for the simple reason that it is small and tough enough to cope with Sicily's mountain roads. Maintenance does not seem high on the Public Works agenda in this part

of the island, so aside from the fact that many roads are not paved, they are also narrow, steep and riddled with potholes.

There is something profound about staying here. You start to understand where Sicily comes from, and why many ancient civilizations tried so hard to take this land. It is not just fertile: it is vast and picturesque. The farmland here is more epic, and more panoramic, than almost anywhere else in Italy. As so few of us have any experience of farming these days, it is also surprisingly interesting and entertaining. The experience, I might say, has also been very nicely rounded out by the conversion of the grain store into a successful restaurant and by the addition of a beautiful pool. As you drive through the remote mountainous landscape on your way to Masseria Susafa, the last thing you would expect to find is a gourmet experience and a turquoise pool with sweeping views.

On various websites Masseria Susafa is described as *agriturismo* – an Italian term for holidays on farms – but the word falls desperately short of the experience. The truth is that here you are the guest of land-owning aristocracy, like the family in *Il Gattopardo*. Hidden in the folds of Sicily's rich and forgotten interior, this farm is a rare survivor from the era of great agricultural estates, the likes of which most people would imagine no longer exist.

It's easy to do nothing at Masseria Susafa – the space and the privacy and the remoteness are all perfectly suited to *far niente*. But it is also well placed to function as a base to explore the Sicilian countryside. It takes less than an hour, for instance, to drive to Piazza Armerina and see first-hand one of the most spectacular Roman mosaics ever found. Leave the farm early in the morning so that you can reward yourself with lunch at nearby Al Fogher, which has been consistently rated as one of the best restaurants in Sicily.

VILLA ROMANA DEL CASALE, PIAZZA ARMERINA

Imago mundi nova...imago nulla.

To think of something new in the
world...is to think of nothing.

IT'S HARD TO BELIEVE, LOOKING AT THESE BIKINI-
CLAD WOMEN – WORKING OUT WITH WEIGHTS, THROWING
A DISCUS, PLAYING BALL GAMES – THAT THIS MOSAIC
FLOOR DATES BACK MORE THAN 1,600 YEARS!

CASTELLO DI FALCONARA

14th-century Fort on a Beach

Castello di Falconara is the real thing: an imposing medieval castle belonging to a baron – Baron Chiaramonte Bordonaro – on the southern coast of Sicily. Built in the 14th century to protect against Barbary pirates, the castle was presented as a gift in 1392 to Ugone di Santapau from King Martin of Aragon as thanks for helping to protect the island from marauding invaders. The name given to this impressive, turreted stone pile stems from a more peaceful later period when the castle was used for hunting; the square tower was where they trained falcons for the hunt. Castello di Falconara changed hands several times over the centuries until the mid-19th century, when it was purchased by the Chiaramonte Bordonaros. The family is mentioned in Raleigh Trevelyan's book *Princes Under the Volcano: Two Hundred Years of a British Dynasty in Sicily* because Charlotte Gardner, the daughter of a British wine distribution scion who had made his fortune in Sicily, married the fabulously wealthy Baron Gabriele Chiaramonte Bordonaro in 1872. (The family's palace in Palermo, Villa Carlotta, is named after her.)

Some years ago, I drove down from Palermo with the current Baron. In keeping with the legacy of the Kingdom of the Two Sicilies, he spoke French. My French, thankfully, was just about good enough to keep up a conversation. It was shocking weather – cloudy, grey and rainy – and I will never forget what he said to me, in a very baron-esque manner: 'Anyone can make this place look good on a sunny day, but only a great photographer can make it look good on a day like today.' It was a challenge, but also a cleverly coded form of encouragement. To be honest, I think Castello di Falconara would look good in any weather. With its hunting trophies from the family's former coffee plantation in Kenya and its extensive, varied collection of handmade tiles, the castle offers a rare insight into a world that has long since disappeared – the rich and aristocratic Sicily of yesteryear.

Apparently, I wasn't the only photographer to appreciate its rare beauty. Shortly after my book, *Hip Hotels Italy*, came out, Mario Testino booked Falconara for a fashion shoot for *Vogue*. Since my last visit, the castle has only got better. The Baron has added a very beautiful swimming pool, nestled among the mature palms that define the garden, and I'm sure the secret internal passageway that he showed me leading directly to the sea – a medieval gem – is now being used by guests to access the beach just below the castle.

AEOLIAN ISLANDS

Seductive Volcanic Dots Untouched by Time

There are seven inhabited islands: Stromboli, Panarea, Alicudi, Filicudi, Lipari, Vulcano and Salina. I have been to six (never managed to get to Alicudi) and stayed on two (Panarea and Salina).

Of the seven, Salina is the most beautiful, the most green, the most mountainous and the most poetic. No wonder it was co-star of the Academy Award-winning film *Il Postino* (1994). Without the island's liltingly romantic, breathtakingly beautiful locations, the film could never have generated such emotion.

The smallest of the inhabited islands is Panarea, which is also quite special, although for very different reasons. It is not epic, like Salina. Rather, it is the very definition of simple. Perfectly simple. It's this quality that appeals to visitors who spend most of the year being exposed to 'too much'.

What all the Aeolian Islands have in common, despite their geographical differences, is their remoteness. These tiny volcanic dots in the Mediterranean are far away from everyone and everything, and there is no easy way to get here. None is big enough for a meaningful landing strip (thank God!), and although there is a helicopter service (Air Panarea), it only operates in the summer and is limited to Panarea. I sincerely hope it stays that way.

The only way to reach the islands is by boat. You can take an overnight ferry from Naples (my preference) or a faster hydrofoil in the summer (four and a half hours of cramped hell – horrible, like a bus, only this bus makes you seasick). You can also catch a ferry from Sicily, which takes around one and a half hours to the island of Salina, although the drive from the airports of Catania or Palermo to the departure port of Milazzo can take a couple of hours or more.

Isolation has ensured the preservation of these islands. Even if they wanted to ramp up their tourism, they can't. And for anyone in search of *la dolce vita*, that's a good thing.

TAKE THE NIGHT BOAT AND WATCH THE SUN RISE OVER STROMBOLI

Siremar, the regular ferry service to the Aeolian Islands, departs twice a week at around 8 p.m. from the passenger terminal in Naples. Judging from the 'Dean Martin goes to Palm Springs' interior, I'm guessing the ship was built in the late 1960s or early '70s – just old enough to be chic again, in a *Wallpaper** magazine 'retro' kind of way. If you go first class, which I would heartily recommend (and it's only marginally more expensive than second class), you get a cabin with a big round porthole, moss-green laminate, mahogany trim, your own mosaic-tiled bathroom and baby-blue linen sheets. I'm sure this is the only ferry on earth to still have linen sheets.

First stop is Stromboli at about 6 a.m., and in the summer this means you will catch the sun rising over the peak of this island's active volcano. That is, if you get out of bed and up on deck early enough. Waking up is not too difficult because the stewards (yes, they still have them) 'gently' knock on all the cabin doors of passengers who are scheduled to alight here. As the ship gets closer to the tiny port, Stromboli's black volcanic beaches come into view with local fishermen dragging their brightly painted wooden boats to the water to start the day's work. You will kick yourself if you miss the sunrise, and the chance to get a *cappu* and a *cornetto alla crema* from the bar to have outside on the top deck, while you watch this tiny volcanic island come to life. It's something you'll never forget.

Next stop is Panarea, roughly an hour and a half by boat from Stromboli. Panarea is relatively flat (its highest peak is less than 500 m) and small (3 km in length) with not much to look at – unless you are gazing back at the smoking silhouette of Stromboli, the views of which happen to be one of Panarea's most significant attractions.

From here the ferry heads to Filicudi, and finally at around 10.30 a.m. it docks at the port of Rinella on the island of Salina. Fourteen and a half hours on the night boat have transported you to a world that few people will ever see or experience.

SIGNUM

Host to Il Postino

In 1994, the world discovered the island of Salina – without ever having been there – because it was the irresistibly seductive setting for the beautiful and heartfelt film, *Il Postino* (which went on to be nominated for five Oscars, winning the award for best score in 1996).

The hero in the film is Mario, a simple man who takes a job delivering mail on his bicycle to the exiled Chilean poet Pablo Neruda, who is in residence on the island. That's how we (the audience) discover the fishing coves of Pollara and the vineyards of the island's lush volcanic centre. Until then, most people, Italians included, had probably never heard of Salina.

Il Postino also helped to create what is, today, one of the best hotels in southern Italy. In the 1990s, an artist named Clara Rametta and her husband Michele set up a small hotel called Signum in a series of renovated stone cottages looking out to sea. In a way it became the de facto HQ for the film, and most of the cast and crew stayed here for the duration of the shoot. When I first visited, a few years after *Il Postino* was released, Clara's hotel had seven rooms, a terrace where breakfast and dinner were served, a small 'inside' restaurant for winter months, and magnificent views of the sea below and Stromboli and Panarea in the distance.

That was then. Today, Signum has some thirty rooms, a beautiful swimming pool, extensive gardens, a separate villa you can rent in its entirety, an acclaimed Michelin-starred restaurant, a 'Roman-style' outdoor, and indoor, geothermal spa, and the best wine list south of Naples – all the while retaining a sense of authenticity. It used to be easy to get a room; now, you must book well in advance. Despite all the success, and having handed over the reins to their children, Clara and Michele's passion for their creation hasn't waned.

Their son Luca, the maître d' of the restaurant and the mastermind behind its formidable Sicilian wine list, has also taken charge of all new work on the interior design and architecture. That's how some rooms now have washbasins chiselled from solid blocks of rough-hewn marble and grey-painted, cast-iron bathtubs standing on traditional *cotto* floors, with views of the sea, while others blend Sicilian wrought-iron furniture with vintage lamps, modern desks and linen couches. No two rooms are the same, and although there's nothing grand about any of them, they all share a tasteful, simple sense of design – a signature, if you will, that is somehow particular to Signum and perfectly in keeping with an unspoilt fishermen's island like Salina.

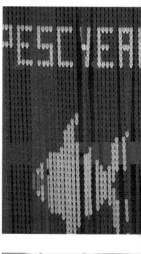

AT THE 68TH ACADEMY AWARDS IN 1996, IL POSTINO WON AN OSCAR FOR BEST ORIGINAL SCORE, BUT EVEN MORE MOVING A

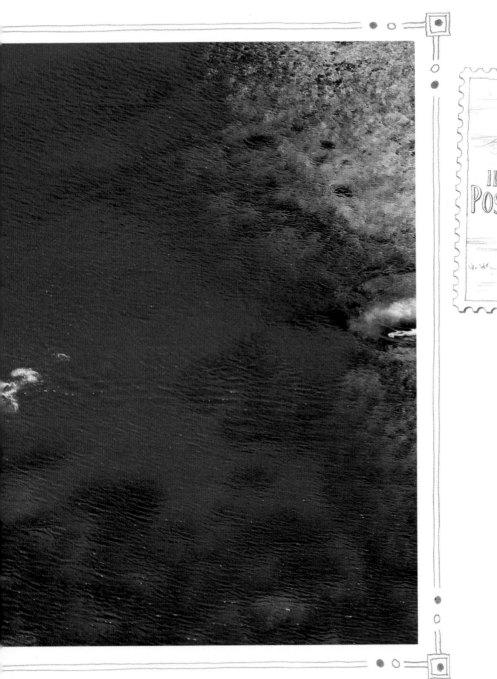

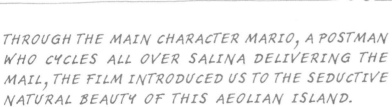

THROUGH THE MAIN CHARACTER MARIO, A POSTMAN
WHO CYCLES ALL OVER SALINA DELIVERING THE
MAIL, THE FILM INTRODUCED US TO THE SEDUCTIVE
NATURAL BEAUTY OF THIS AEOLIAN ISLAND.

NAPLES

Casa D'Anna

Museo Archeologico Nazionale

Casa di Anna

Mattozzi

Terrazza Calabritto

Excelsior

NAPLES

NEAPOLIS – THE GREEK NAME FOR NAPLES – WAS ANCIENT ROME'S FAVOURITE GREEK CITY. THE GREEK LANGUAGE CONTINUED TO FLOURISH HERE EVEN UNDER ROMAN RULE BECAUSE IT WAS 'CHIC TO BE GREEK'.

THE BAY OF NAPLES – DEPICTED HERE BY THE ANCIENT GREEK SYMBOL OF THE CRESCENT AND STAR – WAS THE LOCATION OF CHOICE FOR PATRICIAN ROMANS AND THEIR SUMMER VILLAS. AFTER A 'CULTURAL INTERMISSION' OF ALMOST TWO MILLENNIA, THIS PICTURESQUE STRETCH OF WATER IS ONCE AGAIN THE MOST SOUGHT-AFTER ADDRESS IN THE ANCIENT CITY.

BAY OF NAPLES

Ancient Rome's
Favourite Greek City

Naples is the flower of paradise,
the last adventure of my life.

Alexandre Dumas

Dumas was right: Naples is an adventure – a historic, cultural and hedonistic adventure. Neapolis, the Greek name given to this outpost of Magna Graecia, was an important port in ancient times. It was such a formidable example of Hellenistic culture that Naples maintained the Greek language even during subsequent Roman rule, when Roman emperors would holiday here in villas by the sea. Splendid frescoes and magnificent mosaic floors discovered in nearby Pompeii attest to the extraordinary heights of artisan skill and sophistication. Despite a 'game of thrones', which has seen the Greeks, the Romans, the Moors, the Normans, the Byzantines, the French, the Spanish and the Vatican rule at different times, the city has always retained its reputation for beauty and pleasure.

Naples has the distinction of being one of the oldest continually inhabited cities in the world, the site of at least twenty-seven centuries of unbroken history. Even Rome hasn't managed that! No wonder its entire inner city is listed as a Unesco World Heritage Site. Yet despite all its history and its beautiful setting on the Bay of Naples, the city is nowhere near as popular as Rome, Florence or Venice when it comes to tourism – thank God! This is one of the few places in Italy where you can wander around without being swamped by tourists. I like the fact that Naples has a reputation for being scary. It has patina, for sure – especially in the oldest part of the city, with its narrow streets and eroded façades – but that doesn't mean it's unsafe. In reality, Naples is no different from any other city, and provided you use your common sense, you are unlikely to run into trouble.

Of course, Naples has plenty to see in terms of museums, ruins and noteworthy sites, but let's assume you've already done 'all that' in Rome and Florence, and Venice too. Instead, why not take advantage of the weather and the beautiful seaside location and do very little except have lunch, go for a swim, and perhaps get some shirts made by the city's legendary tailors. Spend a few relaxed, agenda-free days wandering around a city that is far more exotic than any in the north.

EXCELSIOR

A Grand Night and an Even Grander View

The Excelsior is a stately stone pile with the very best location in Naples, on the corner of the seaside corniche with an uninterrupted view of the Bay of Naples. It's a grand establishment with high ceilings, a sweeping marble staircase and a lobby straight out of an Agatha Christie novel. This is old Italy at its 'slightly worn around the edges', aristocratic best. A small army of ultra-smart waiters, permanently dressed in black tie (white jackets in the morning, black after dark), caters to your every whim. In the warmer months (April to November) breakfast is served on the roof, which offers a stunning vista of the azure blue Mediterranean, Vesuvius and the islands of Ischia and Capri in the distance. The hotel faces onto Via Partenope, a recently pedestrianized street that skirts the sea and is a popular place for an evening *passeggiata*.

The Excelsior's buzzing location and 'old world' style make it the place to stay in Naples. And the good news is that a night here costs less than a room in a third-rate hotel in Venice.

LUNCH IN A SECRET COURTYARD...
THE BEST-KEPT SECRET IN NAPLES.

THIS UNASSUMING PIZZERIA, SITUATED BEHIND
THE IRON GATES OF A PATRICIAN TOWNHOUSE
IN THE HEART OF OLD NAPLES, IS WITHOUT
DOUBT THE BEST RESTAURANT IN TOWN.

MUSEO ARCHEOLOGICO NAZIONALE

The Most Important Archaeological Museum in the World

The terrible disaster that befell Pompeii and Herculaneum nearly 2,000 years ago, when Mount Vesuvius exploded into a giant ball of fire and ash, has today provided us with an extraordinarily accurate glimpse of our ancient past. The lava and volcanic dust that quickly buried these towns also helped to preserve them. Without the evidence of daily life unearthed at these sites, we would have little idea of the Romans' elaborate sense of colour or their predilection for extravagant decorative detail in everything from floors and walls to household objects.

Yet this is not what you will see if you visit Pompeii. That's because most of it, certainly the best of it – including the frescoed walls, floor mosaics, busts, statues, and even tableware – reside in a series of monumental halls that constitute the Museo Archeologico Nazionale in the old centre of Naples. No wonder, then, that it is considered by many to be the most important archaeological museum in the world. Nowhere else can match it in terms of the quantity, quality and diversity of its ancient artefacts. In the halls that house statue after statue, a parade of Roman 'celebrities' is on display: influential senators, pudgy-faced aristocrats, hawk-nosed writers and effeminate poets, powerfully muscular heroes such as Hercules, fashionable ladies and various Roman Caesars. And for anyone with even a passing interest in decoration or design, there are vast spaces dedicated to extraordinary housewares – glasses, cups, plates, bowls and trays so well preserved they almost appear contemporary. There are massive, ballroom-sized spaces dedicated to mosaics, and another floor of equally large rooms filled with Pompeian walls painted with richly elaborate vistas that are testament to the startling Roman preference for deep crimson reds, chalky muted blacks, vivid warm yellows and strong greens.

In the introduction to this chapter, I said that Naples is the kind of city you should wander around without agenda and it's true: the city is best viewed with spontaneity, with one exception – the Museo Archeologico Nazionale. It will take you on an adventure into life in ancient Rome; children (even teenagers) will find themselves drawn into it. The best frescoes and mosaics from Herculaneum and Pompeii, and the most beautiful Roman statues, are here to be admired without queues or crowds.

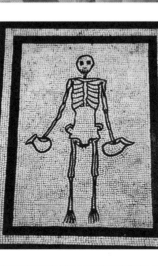

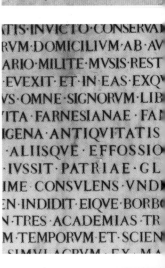

TERRAZZA CALABRITTO

A Table with a View

In ancient times, aristocratic citizens of Rome maintained sprawling summer villas on the picturesque Bay of Naples. These privileged Roman 'escapees' loved Neapolis because it was so chic...and so Greek. Despite being part of the Roman Empire, Neapolis retained its Greek identity, and Greek was still the language being spoken because Romans preferred it that way. The Romans liked the old language because it was considered more worldly than Latin. Neapolis was Rome's Riviera – a cosmopolitan retreat built *pieds dans l'eau* on the turquoise blue Mediterranean, and Rome's beau monde visited at every opportunity.

But as with most European cities situated on the sea, subsequent civilizations saw the centre move further and further away from the shore. Being by the sea was only desirable if you were a fisherman or dockworker. Only today – some sixteen centuries after the fall of Rome – is the Bay of Naples starting to make a comeback. The street running along the water's edge – the famous Via Partenope – has been closed to

traffic for a number of years and is now a popular destination for an evening *passeggiata*. Locals with their families stroll along the boulevard (way past most people's bedtime) to take in the cooler sea air. It was only a matter of time before contemporary style and taste followed this relatively new passion for the seaside geographic. In a way, Terrazzo Calabritto is proof that the Bay of Naples is experiencing a genuine Renaissance.

All new, in a chic 'neo-fifties' kind of way, with grey velvet chairs and lamps that evoke Saturn, Terrazza Calabritto on Piazza Vittoria – from which Via Partenope starts – has a splendid view of the Bay of Naples, a menu that includes spaghetti with crab and sea bass baked in a crust of sea salt, and a reputation that has made it the talk of the town. (Well, you can't eat every meal at Mattozzi!) Terrazza Calabritto is handsome, stylish and sophisticated, and it offers something that until relatively recently was impossible to get in Naples: lunch with a view of the sea, just as it was in Roman times.

CASA DI ANNA

B&B in an Authentic Inner-city Palazzo

It wasn't easy to find. The heart of historic Naples is labyrinthine and dense, and Google Maps wasn't much help; but asking lots of locals was. Eventually, my children and I arrived at a set of immense doors, covered in graffiti, which, strangely, proved quite an attractive and successful foil for the inner-city palazzo's imposing entrance. It made it more interesting and inviting, especially given the dark, foreboding space that followed. The porte cochère – the vaulted stretch immediately following the entrance – was rather dim and uninspiring, as was the internal courtyard. Originally built as a space for a horse and carriage to turn around, it felt and looked like it had not been used properly for at least a hundred years. Tucked subtly into one corner (almost hidden) was a slender stone staircase sporting a single classical statue in the bend of its landing. It was the kind of staircase that could easily feature in a Visconti film. Upon arrival on the first floor, there were only two choices: a door on the left and a very heavy, reinforced steel door on the right. The steel one had a tiny sign that read Casa di Anna, so I rang it and the steel barrier crept open to reveal a young lady in an unexpectedly modern, light-filled space.

It was the type of contrast that makes travelling in Italy so worthwhile. Here was a completely unexpected series of clean, contemporary spaces hidden in the hulk of a long-forgotten inner-city palazzo. The only real connection to the past that remained was the scale: the impressive ceiling height and the old-fashioned huge size of the rooms. The rooms were bright, simple and spacious, with ultra-modern en-suite bathrooms, and there was a communal kitchen perfectly suited to the breakfast part of the 'bed and breakfast' equation. The young lady standing in the entrance proved to be the daughter of the owner, and she must have thought me very odd because I kept asking her if her Scottish and French friends were also around.

I had read about Casa D'Anna (notice the slightly different spelling?) in a French fashion magazine a few months earlier. It described a small bed and breakfast in a baroque palazzo – not far from the Museo Archeologico Nazionale – as a joint venture between an Italian, a Scot and a Frenchman, and went on to praise it as much for its affordability as for its sense of style. Who would have thought there would be two places with virtually the same name in Naples? Both in an old palazzo. Both stylishly converted into affordable bed-and-breakfast accommodation. Amazingly, I had managed to find the one that hadn't been written about.

AMALFI
COAST

Pastel Villages Perched Above the Sea

Ravello, Sorrento, Positano... The names roll off the tongue with anticipation, conjuring up images of timeless pastel-coloured fishing villages clinging to impossibly steep granite slopes high above the vivid blue Mediterranean. No part of Italy is as synonymous with *la dolce vita* as the Amalfi Coast.

For millennia, travellers have been captivated by this coastline. Richard Wagner, M. C. Escher, Greta Garbo, Virginia Woolf, Gore Vidal, Joan Miró, Truman Capote, Tennessee Williams, Graham Greene, Jacqueline Kennedy and Leonard Bernstein all indulged in its sun-kissed, lemon-scented lifestyle and spectacular natural beauty. So enamoured was John Steinbeck that, in 1953, he wrote a piece titled 'Positano' for *Harper's Bazaar*.

These are the parts of Italy immortalized in Homer's *Odyssey*, and for good reason. Where else in the Mediterranean would you place the islands of the sirens, whose sweet singing lured sailors towards the rocks and certain death?

SAMPLE
THE GRAPHIC
GENIUS OF
GIO PONTI

Gio Ponti was a one-man creative machine. He founded *Domus*, arguably the world's most famous architecture and design magazine. He designed some of Italy's most iconic examples of modernity, including Milan's Pirelli Tower, and he created a chair – the aptly named Superleggera – that still ranks among the most enduringly popular of Italian designs, which in itself is really saying something. Ponti was the Italian version of Frank Lloyd Wright, especially in his multidisciplinary range of interests and the substantial legacy he left behind. He is lauded as the most influential figure in 20th-century Italian modernism.

Perhaps the most focused and singular of all his work was the design he came up with at the request of a Neapolitan engineer, Roberto Fernandes. Completed in 1962, Parco dei Principi hotel in Sorrento – which was built on the site of an unfinished Gothic structure, in the former grounds of the 18th-century Villa Siracusa – is perched on a monumen-tal cliff overlooking the sea. The story behind Ponti's design scheme was one of 'magnificent restraint'. Inspired by the extraordinary setting, Ponti opted for a starkly geometric, all-white design with an interior scheme that used just one colour: blue. Blue phones, blue fabric, blue blinds, blue ceramics, blue lift doors...and, most importantly, blue floors, made up of blue tiles in countless patterns that Ponti designed himself. The geometric blue tiles he created were not only boldly graphic but also beauti-fully appropriate – echoing both the colour of the Mediterranean and the Neapolitan tradition of tile-making.

Decades later, the bold angular lines of the hotel's whitewashed exterior and the 'all blue' interior continue to draw visitors from around the world. Parco dei Principi still looks fresh and adventurously modern, and – if any proof were needed of Ponti's timeless talent – repro-ductions of the tiles are now available to buy. A good story, and an even better souvenir.

LA MINERVETTA

The Most Stylish Address in Sorrento

Minerva was the Roman goddess of wisdom and – through her association with her Greek equivalent, Athena – strategic warfare. Minervetta means 'little Minerva', a reference to the limited number of rooms at this hotel (there are just twelve).

Of all the hotels in Sorrento, La Minervetta has the best location, high above the town, and the best views. From the terrace that is used to serve breakfast, an expanse of blue stretches out into the distance, broken only by the silhouette of Mount Vesuvius against the skyline.

The Amalfi Coast carries certain expectations – a fantasy, if you will – and La Minervetta delivers on that fantasy. Its interiors are exactly how you would imagine a boutique hotel in such a magical setting to look – bright and whitewashed, and decorated with bold, fresh stripes in different shades of blue. Add to this the high ceilings, the extraordinary collection of illustrated books – which make the living area feel more like a glamorous library – and the assortment of quirky decorative items, ranging from model ships to 1980s Memphis vases, and you have a signature style that is fabulous and fun.

For the architect-owner Marco de Luca, stylish is normal. He worked for many years as an interior designer in Florence before returning to Sorrento – plus he is half Danish, so the clean, pared-down look is in his blood! At La Minervetta, you feel like you are a guest in an architect's private apartment that just happens to have the most perfect location on the Amalfi Coast, which is near enough the truth.

EXPLORE THE GARDENS OF VILLA CIMBRONE

Ernest William Beckett, second Baron Grimthorpe, didn't do much right in his life. He was a notorious gambler and womanizer, he was kicked out of his family's bank for reckless spending, and he was forced to sell the family estate to cover his many debts. But, in 1904, one thing he did do that cannot be faulted was to buy a ruined farmhouse in Ravello, which he trans-formed in a magnificently exotic and eccentric manner that only the most decadent of British aristocracy seemed to get away with. With the help of Nicola Mansi, a local barber-builder, he created a fantasy: a palace with towers and battlements expressed in an odd but somehow convincing mix of Moorish, Venetian and Gothic styles. And from a paddock that had once been

used by monks to graze cows, between the cliff's edge and the house, he created a garden with Moorish tea houses and grottoes and classical statues and pavilions, in a similarly eclectic style as the house.

The garden, which is now open to the public, is particularly renowned for its spectacular belvedere, the Terrazzo dell'Infinito (Terrace of Infinity). This is a panorama to beat all panoramas, a fact that has not been lost on Hollywood. John Huston chose to feature it in his 1953 film *Beat the Devil* starring Humphrey Bogart, and more recently, if you watch the trailer for Marvel's *Wonder Woman* (2017) you will see the belvedere in all its cinematic glory.

Lord Grimthorpe passed away in 1917, but his descendants managed to hang on to Villa Cimbrone, his creation, until the 1960s, when it was sold to the Vuilleumier family; they used it as a summer house and later transformed it into a luxurious hotel, which is what it is today. In the interim years, when Villa Cimbrone still belonged to a Beckett, it played host to many famous names. Virginia Woolf, D. H. Lawrence, Henry Moore, T. S. Eliot, Jean Piaget, Winston Churchill and, most famously, Greta Garbo, who came here to escape from the press (not very successfully as there were journalists continually camped at the gates), were all much enamoured with Lord Grimthorpe's 'folly', and with the town of Ravello.

Ravello is poised nearly 400 m above sea level and, as such, it is removed from the hustle and bustle of the coast. It is quieter and calmer and far less touristy than other places, which is no doubt part of its enduring appeal. This is the sort of place you would come to paint or write – or simply to think.

The winged valkyries were warrior women of Norse legend who would choose which battle-slain heroes to take to Valhalla.

THE TERRACE OF INFINITY IS A PANORAMA TO BEAT ALL PANORAMAS. IT WAS WAGNER'S INSPIRATION FOR *RIDE OF THE VALKYRIES*, HUSTON'S SETTING FOR

JOHN HUSTON'S
"BEAT THE DEVIL"

HUMPHREY BOGART

JENNIFER JONES

GINA LOLLOBRIGIDA

The shield of
Wonder Woman

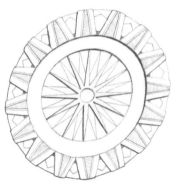

HIS 1953 ADVENTURE FILM *BEAT THE DEVIL*, AND
MORE RECENTLY THE HOLLYWOOD STAND-IN FOR WONDER
WOMAN'S AMAZONIAN ISLAND IN THE 2017 MOVIE.

LE SIRENUSE

Legendary Hotel in a Former Summer Palace

The first time I stayed at Le Sirenuse in Positano, I was the guest of Antonio Sersale, whose father Franco – together with his three siblings – had transformed this noble family's summer palace into a hotel in the early 1950s. But the hotel was overbooked on my first night, so I stayed in a house next door with Franco, who also happened to be a photographer. Franco would have liked to travel more, but for a large part of his life he had to be here to manage and look after the family business. In 1992 Antonio took over the reins, along with the obligations.

You see how it works. There's a certain *noblesse oblige* to this business. Managing the Sersale family's former summer palace brings with it certain privileges; you get to meet interesting people from around the world and eat fine food, for example. But it also carries responsibilities, which probably outweigh the privileges. This is by no means a business set up solely to make money. It may be called a hotel, but in every sense it is still the Sersales' ancestral family home, which makes anyone who stays here a de facto house guest.

Yes, it has the best location in Positano and the restaurant is the best in town, and of course it helps from an aesthetic point of view that this was a summer palace for Neapolitan nobility. But it's the fact that it's a family business passed from one Sersale to the next which ensures its longevity: each generation tries to do better than the one before it, and that's why Le Sirenuse is the best hotel on the Amalfi Coast.

Even if you are not staying at Le Sirenuse, it should still be on your list of places to eat. Italian food is not about innovation, but about quality – the quality of the ingredients. A *prosciutto e melone*, for example, perfect for the summer temperatures of the Amalfi Coast, is only as good as the ham and melon that are used to make it. It's a simple but important logic that can be applied to almost every summer dish. In the world of Italian cuisine, who you are matters, and how long you've been around – it affects your ability to get the best ingredients from the best suppliers. In these parts nobody has been around longer or is better connected than the Sersale family. End of story.

CAPRI

Fashionable Fleck in the Mediterranean

Like the sirens in Homer's *Odyssey*, whose rocky home is widely believed to have been inspired by the island, Capri holds a beguiling attraction that has drawn people to it for centuries – from emperors and royalty to writers and stars of the silver screen. So enthralled was the Roman emperor Tiberius when he visited in AD 27 that he never left, ruling the entire empire from a sumptuous villa built high on a peak that now bears his name.

All the fuss could easily have ruined Capri, but it hasn't. Against the odds, this fashionable fleck in the Mediterranean has managed to stay true to its stylish self. That is because, first and foremost, Capri is an escape for Italians, the type of Italians portrayed in the film *La Grande Bellezza* – chic and successful, largely from the worlds of art, design and fashion, but with a mix of the aristocratic elite and the crème de la crème of business. They are people with a zest for life, an eye for style and an appreciation of the finer things. And on Capri, the 'finer things' means the 'simpler things', like walking down the steps from Punta di Tragara to the sea for a pre-breakfast swim or strolling into town for a coffee on the charming Piazzetta.

It is hard to imagine a more idyllic place or a more perfect start to the day. During the summer months, the sun comes out like clockwork with not a cloud in the sky. By the time that the ferries and cruise ships start to unload their passengers, the 'summer residents' – a handy catchphrase that applies to anyone staying on the island, even if it's just for a few days – have retreated to their understated hotels and bougainvillea-clad houses. Just before lunch, they re-emerge, but only to go down to the beach clubs, situated far away from the touristy harbour. Towards the end of the afternoon, the day visitors are obliged to catch the last ferries back to the mainland and Capri is once more in the hands of the *cognoscenti*. The summer residents slip on their handmade sandals and head back into town, bronzed and elegantly dressed, for an *aperitivo* at one of the many bars and cafés that have returned to the old order.

Perhaps it's because everything about Capri is consistently beautiful or the fact that the rhythm of life is so perfectly in step with summer, but there is something strangely seductive at play here that is definitely more than the sum of its parts. Millennia after Homer wrote his epic, this captivating island in the Mediterranean has lost none of its allure – the spirit of the sirens lives on.

GET A BOAT OF YOUR OWN

The trick to extracting the most from this gorgeous speck in the sea is to mimic the lifestyle of the Italians who holiday here every summer. And that means getting a boat of your own – even if only for one day. Nothing fancy, mind you. I am not talking about chartering a 'gin palace' or one of those glamorous mahogany speedboats that cost more than a house. I'm talking about hiring one of the traditional boats that have been fishing these waters for centuries, a *gozzo caprese*. These small but seaworthy craft can get very close to the rocky shores, and dart in and out of the coves and caves without difficulty. Many *gozzi* have been converted from fishing duty to 'pleasure craft' simply by putting a mattress-cum-daybed over the space that used

to hold the fish. And normally, when you hire one for the day, it comes with a boat boy – a local who steers the boat, operates the engine and knows the island like the back of his hand. Or, if you're game, you can hire a smaller *lancia* and steer yourself (this is certainly cheaper, starting at around 70 euros, as opposed to 400 euros per day for a manned *gozzo*).

Hiring a boat of your own should be an activity without agenda. The only decision you will have to face is whether to make your way around the island in a clockwise or anticlockwise direction. I would recommend clockwise; it feels more natural and you will be in sync with the movement of the sun. Having established the direction, you can retire to your daybed and point at places you want to explore, stopping wherever you want for a swim in the clear waters surrounding the island.

You are likely, of course, to pass the famous Grotta Azzurra (Blue Grotto), but I would avoid getting closer unless it is very early in the morning. For most of the day the cave is clogged with tourists packed onto overcrowded bus-like boats waiting their turn – not exactly a magical experience, and one that is almost certain to break the sirens' spell. Far better, because it is quieter, is the Grotta Verde (Green Grotto) on the other side of the island. It is so much further from the Marina Grande that it is far less busy.

One important thing to remember about having a boat of your own is that it is not a 'guided' experience. The idea isn't to ask your boat boy a question every few minutes. If you do, you run the risk of being bombarded with banal detail for the rest of the day. If you watch the locals, you will notice that they do not speak to the boat boy unless it is to give directions: 'Stop, I want to swim here!' There is a knack, you see, to being a successful hedonist, and the best way to learn is by imitation.

CASA MALAPARTE

A View that is Worthy of Homer

As you navigate your way around Capri, you will pass a house that has become an object of pilgrimage for architects the world over. Perched 32 m above the sea, Casa Malaparte famously featured in Jean-Luc Godard's *Contempt* (*Le Mépris*) of 1963. Starring Brigitte Bardot as a screenwriter's wife whose marriage is disintegrating, and Jack Palance as a hot-headed, salacious American producer who is trying to make a film of Homer's *Odyssey*, *Contempt* is set almost entirely in and around Casa Malaparte. And despite the fact that Bardot is at the peak of her blonde magnificence, and those scenes of her swimming naked in the clear waters of the Mediterranean, the real stars are Casa Malaparte and Capri.

Built on what is often described as an 'impossible' spot, Casa Malaparte was designed by Italian architect Adalberto Libera in 1937 as a summer house for the controversial author and intellectual Curzio Malaparte. It is still disputed, to this day, if Libera should really take the credit for the house because Malaparte claimed that he rejected Libera's design and built the house himself with the help of his stonemason. Whoever deserves the credit, one thing is clear: it is an extraordinary house in an equally extraordinary location. What is particularly clever is how Casa Malaparte has achieved such a strong unity with its setting, without resorting to predictable organic shapes. Instead, it borrows from local traditions and ancient Mediterranean cultures. Viewed from the side, it resembles a typical village house with its thick walls and slanted roof. From the back, it is more like something the ancient Greeks would have built: a monumental set of steps climbs gradually to an open outdoor space (the roof), with unencumbered, breathtaking views on all sides. Only a curved wall stands, like a backdrop, on the otherwise open space, which makes it look and feel like a temple or a place for a play...or a sacrifice.

What I really love about this house is how impossible it is to get to. Reaching the house by sea can be done but requires skilful navigation of the rocky shores below and stamina to climb the famous 99 steps that are cut into the cliff. There are no roads, just narrow pathways, so the only alternative is to traverse the island on foot. Starting from Capri's Piazzetta (Piazza Umberto I), it takes an hour and a half to walk, and for the last twenty minutes of the journey you are on private land belonging to the Ronchi Foundation, which owns and maintains the house. This is what I mean when I say that Capri has stayed true to itself: no amount of money can make the island sacrifice its natural beauty.

HIKE TO THE EMPEROR TIBERIUS' RUINS

Tiberius, successor to and stepson of Augustus, was not a very popular or effective emperor. The great-uncle of Caligula and great-granduncle of Nero was described as a dark and sombre ruler, but the one thing that made him stand out was that he abandoned Rome in favour of the isle of Capri. He ruled the entire Roman Empire for almost eleven years (AD 27–37) from the remote magnificence of the 7,000 m² Villa Jovis (Villa Jupiter) on what is now Mount Tiberius, with a panoramic view of Naples, Mount Vesuvius, Ischia and the Bay of Salerno. You can visit the ruins of the villa if you're up for the forty-five-minute, two-mile hike from the Piazzetta. A series of narrow trails and fragrant pathways lead to the site, and on the way you will pass Villa Lysis, a neoclassical villa of the early 1900s made famous by the scandalized French author and aristocrat Count Jacques d'Adelswärd-Fersen, as well as the lesser-known Parco Astarita, where you can walk among wild goats while admiring the view.

When you finally arrive at Villa Jovis, it is impossible not to be impressed with the setting and the scale. From the reconstructive drawings that show the massive complex as it may have looked, it is clear that Tiberius was a man of taste, but to gain some insight into his character you need only seek out the vantage point known as 'Tiberius' Leap', with its 300-m drop to the sea below. This is where disobedient servants and unfortunate guests are said to have been given a simple choice: jump or be pushed!

LA FONTELINA

The Best Beach Club

It might not seem particularly original to write about La Fontelina as Capri's best beach club. It hardly needs the attention. With its own website, an online illustrated book, and a formidable list of famous faces who have sunned themselves, bathed and lunched here over the years, it would have been easy for La Fontelina to become a little spoiled, jaded, too big for its boots – but nothing could be further from the truth.

For a place that is written about so often, it is strange how seldom it seems to be found! That's probably because everyone ends up at Da Luigi instead. I did, the first few times I took the steep and winding path down from Punta di Tragara. Da Luigi, another famous beach club, lies at the very end of the path and so, logically, that's where you stop. Not that there's anything wrong with doing so. Da Luigi has great seafood, lots of daybeds and umbrellas, and plenty of ladders to swim from – everything you could want from a Capri beach club...except it's not as special as La Fontelina. To get to La Fontelina, you have to make the extra effort. At the bottom of the path, just before Da Luigi, you turn right and follow a rudimentary track over the craggy rocks that define the shore.

At first glance, La Fontelina is not much more than a collection of blue-and-white umbrellas dotted among the rocks, with tables and chairs arranged under a bamboo awning set for lunch; there are a handful of ladders plunging into natural rock pools. It looks like it could be washed away by the next storm, and occasionally, especially during the winter months, it is. But this is all part of the charm. La Fontelina is simple and unpretentious, and the experience is the same whether you're a billionaire or the average punter.

Plenty of magazines, newspapers and journals have waxed lyrical about La Fontelina and the view. La Fontelina looks out over the mythical Faraglioni, the vertical rocks that the blinded Cyclops angrily hurled at Odysseus in Homer's *Odyssey*. But strangely, the glowing reviews seem to miss the one ingredient that really makes La Fontelina so special, and that is family. La Fontelina is operated by family, and always has been – one look at the photos on the website will tell you that. Do they show an endless parade of celebrities? They could do, but they don't. The photos are of sons, daughters, grandparents, uncles, aunts, cousins, nephews and nieces of the family who work here. This is where the enduring magic of La Fontelina lies. It still feels like you have crashed a fisherman's family lunch.

FRANK SANG ABOUT IT, HOMER WROTE ABOUT IT, BARDOT SCANDALIZED IT,

HURCHILL PAINTED IT, GODARD FILMED IT... NO WONDER,

THEN, THAT CAPRI IS THE MOST FAMOUS FLECK IN THE MEDITERRANEAN.

PUNTA TRAGARA

Le Corbusier on Capri

At the end of a long, narrow path that winds from the town to a promontory known as Punta di Tragara sits a hotel of the same name. Hotel Punta Tragara is the place I would choose for myself and recommend to friends every time. It may not be the grandest hotel on the island, or the most famous, but it is, in my opinion, the best. I say this for many reasons.

Situated far from town, on the opposite side of the island to the Marina Grande, Hotel Punta Tragara enjoys one of the quietest and most secluded locations on Capri – and once you see the sheer volume of day visitors that arrive here in summer, you will realize just how important this is. It is also perched, like an eagle's nest, on the edge of a cliff, with spectacular sea views and an unencumbered vista of the famous Faraglioni stacks far below. The fact that the steps leading from the hotel's front door also lead to the best beach club on the island is an added bonus.

And then there are some qualities that are equally poignant but not so obvious, such as the fact that the hotel was originally designed by Le Corbusier, in the 1920s, as a villa for Emilio Errico Vismara, an engineer from Lombardy.

Le Corbusier intended Villa Vismara to be 'an extension of the rock', and in this he succeeded admirably. It is everything you would expect of this famously intuitive architect, who travelled around the Mediterranean with his sketchbook in lieu of a more formal education.

Le Corbusier's 'being one with the rock' mantra was certainly not lost on the Allied Forces who chose to take a leaf from Tiberius' book and made Villa Vismara home to the American command during the Second World War. Famous guests, predictably, included General Eisenhower and Winston Churchill.

In 1968, Count Goffredo Manfredi purchased the house as a summer residence. When he decided to transform the house into a hotel, in 1973, some of Le Corbusier's signature was unavoidably watered down by the subsequent expansion. What the site never lost, and retains to this day, however, is the modern master's legendary talent for making the most of a location.

Punta Tragara, as a hotel, is refined, understated and elegant, like Capri itself. The food is wonderful, the rooms are suitably sophisticated and stylish, but it is the view and location that will always remain the star attraction.

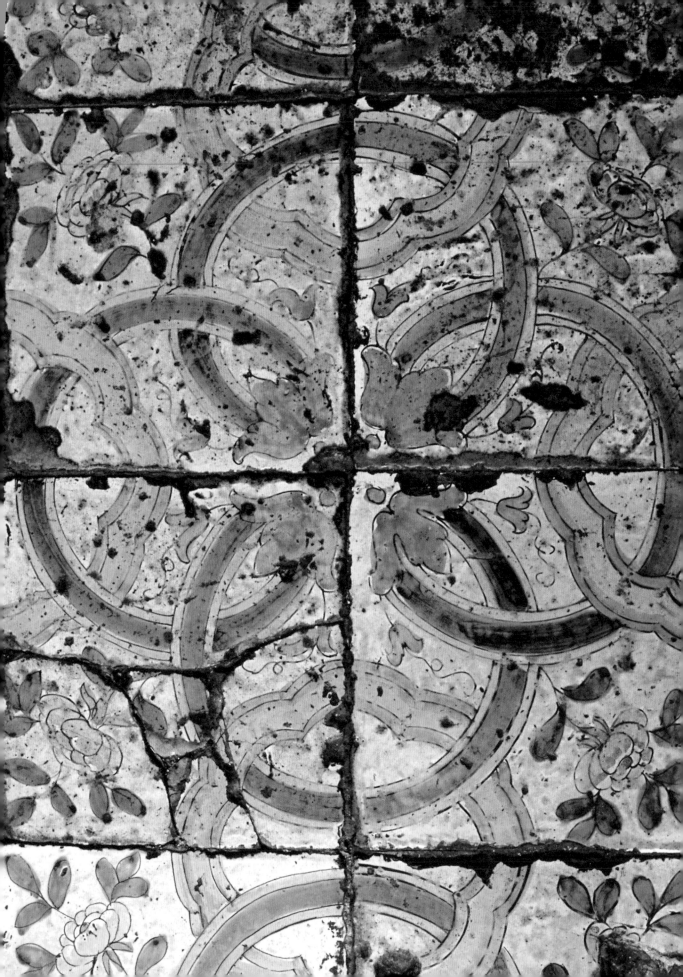

MATERA

Back to
the Bible

If you've seen the most recent cinematic adaptation of *Ben-Hur* (2016), you know what Matera looks like, because it was filmed here. Matera is how you imagine biblical Jerusalem to have looked, and of all the places to visit in Italy this is not one to miss. It is a fascinating testament to human endurance, a city that opens our eyes to man's evolution from cave-dweller to church-builder to New World emigrant.

Matera's story is not one of greatness, but an epic tale of survival – of making do with nothing for thousands of years; and when, finally, 'nothing' proved too much, entire families left to try their luck in America. This is not a place where great dynasties such as the Medici tried their 'monumental' best to please God, but where generation after generation played out a dire existence that begged the question: does God really exist? If nothing else, as Carlo Levi so eloquently argues, its 'sorrowful beauty' will make you think.

The story does have a happy ending though, of sorts. The city lost many people to famine, pestilence, poverty and emigration, but fast-forward to today, and Matera – with the help of Unesco and Hollywood – is in the middle of a substantial revival.

EXPLORE THE HOLLYWOOD 'STAND-IN' FOR JERUSALEM

So many films – from *King David* (1985), which starred Richard Gere, to *The Passion of the Christ* (2004), directed by Mel Gibson, to *The Young Messiah* (2016) and even *The Omen* (2006) and *Wonder Woman* (2017) – have made use of the ancient, primeval-looking scenery of Matera and its surroundings. It seems to be Hollywood's favourite 'stand-in' for ancient Judea. That's because it doesn't just look authentic – it is authentic. You don't need props to transform this town of caves and churches and simple stone houses into a biblical setting because it has changed very little since the birth of Christ. Centuries of abject poverty and neglect have preserved the appearance of Matera, making it not just rare but irreplaceable. There is perhaps only one other place in the world that feels similarly biblical, in my view, and that's Tigmi. This tiny town in the foothills of the Atlas mountains, not far from Marrakesh, doesn't have electricity, and the people still get around on donkeys; it is also where Martin Scorsese filmed *The Last Temptation of Christ*.

You'll no longer find donkeys at Matera, and considering the speed with which the city is being 'fixed up' and the swarm of building cranes on the horizon, I wonder if the aura of 'ancient Judea' will last. There's a danger that the current zeal for restoration will destroy the very quality that makes Matera so convincing – which is all the more reason to make it part of your Italy itinerary, and soon.

As Richard Gere said, although *King David* was a flop, 'I'd do it all over again, because it gave me the opportunity to discover Matera, which I would never have otherwise got to know.'

LE GROTTE DELLA CIVITA

Caves Unchanged Since the Dawn of Man

Not long ago, Matera was the shame of Italy. When the Italian Prime Minister visited here in the 1950s, it was one of the poorest and most unhealthy places on the planet. The infant mortality rate was medieval, tuberculosis was rife and life expectancy was low. The Italian government was compelled to act and built an entirely new Matera – a shiny, modern one – on the other side of the mountain. People who had been living with their animals in caves, using their dung and manure as fuel to generate heat, were moved into brand-new apartments. Many left their rudimentary, handmade possessions, such as rough, rugged tables and benches, behind in the caves.

Who would ever have imagined that these same objects – these poignant reminders of tragic poverty – would one day feature as essential pieces of a hotel experience? Swedish–Italian entrepreneur, hotelier and philanthropist Daniele Kihlgren saw the potential when he bought a series of abandoned *sassi* (caves) in Matera facing the Gravina (a ravine carved by what was once a powerful river), with a view to creating an *albergo diffuso*, a hotel that would evoke the 'soul' of these former dwellings. The *sassi* were the very first human settlement in Italy – prehistoric cave drawings have been found here – and it is this extraordinary legacy that Kihlgren wanted to celebrate with a completely original experience.

He wanted guests to be able to experience living in a cave of primordial ambience and origin, without denying them the luxury and comfort of modern amenities.

This was a tall order: the authenticity of an ancient cave dwelling without any of the discomfort. But that's exactly what he delivered in 2009 with the opening of Le Grotte della Civita. He deserves a medal for his unprecedented, inspired approach – and for his persistence. The first step in an extraordinarily laborious process was to strip the eighteen caves back to their most basic origins, uncovering the original stone floors and walls, no matter how uneven or damaged. These stone floors were carefully excavated to allow wiring, plumbing and heating to be fitted underneath before putting the original floors back, warts and all. Alcoves and natural divisions were cleverly used to hide away the toilets and bathrooms.

Then it was time to address the furniture and furnishings. Repaired, but not restored was the *modus operandi*, and all the rough, uneven, battered, chipped and gouged tables and benches – left behind in the caves and untouched for decades – were then incorporated into the design of the guest caves. It sounds like an odd thing to do, but it had one thing going for it: it was authentic. To this 'arte povera', Kihlgren added handmade bedspreads woven on traditional

looms and thick, coarse linen tablecloths in natural colours, along with beeswax candles, plain earthenware and dim lighting that is strategically hidden away from view – all in an effort to respect the original shape and materials of the *sassi* and to evoke the cultural and human history of this place in a meaningful way.

It is one thing to stomp around the city as a visitor, but quite another to stay here in a manner unchanged for thousands of years. That's the magic of Le Grotte della Civita. I stayed for two nights in Cave 11, and I can vouch that all the work that went into this Sextantio was worth it, three times over. It feels right, in Matera, to be staying in a cave – in the same way that it feels right to stay on a farm in Sicily, or in a palazzo on a canal in Venice. It becomes so much more memorable because you are at one with your environment. And it's not just the uneven floors and ruggedly handsome aesthetic of your cave: it's a layering of different details and experiences.

The view into the Gravina – a sweeping vista of an ancient landscape that evolves from a cold bluish tone in the morning to a harsh, sunscorched patina at midday to a golden, almost orange tone at sunset – has a similar effect.

Even breakfast is nothing like you will ever have experienced before. The largest cave – which is taller and more monumental than the others because it was once used as a place of worship – is the unexpected setting for the first meal of the day: a 'deconsecrated church' set with rough tables and rugged benches and coarse linen tablecloths and uneven white pottery for a breakfast that is as plentiful and delicious as the space is spartan and pious. Here, contrast becomes a powerful tool.

In a strange, almost covert way, the shame of Italy has become the pride of Italy, with a story of survival – a very human tale – at its heart. If that's not the real *dolce vita*, then I don't know what is.

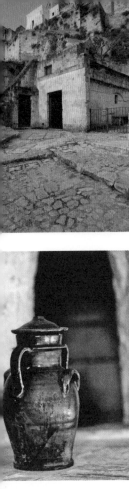

PUGLIA

PUGLIA

ADRIATIC SEA

PUGLIA'S CHRISTIAN CULTURE STRETCHES BACK MANY CENTURIES, TO WHEN THE REGION WAS PART OF THE BYZANTINE EMPIRE. APPROPRIATELY, THE ARMS OF A BYZANTINE CROSS PINPOINT THE BEST THAT THIS WHITEWASHED, SUNBURNT LAND HAS TO OFFER.

Bari

Alberobello

Masseria Alchimia

Brindisi

Lecce

Masseria Prosperi

Otranto

Convento di Santa Maria di Costantinopoli

Lo Scalo

SALENTO COAST

IONIAN SEA

n g

Ancient, Whitewashed and Sunburnt

Puglia is a land of pale blue Adriatic waters, rich red soil, timeless seaside villages and a history that makes it one of the oldest parts of Italy. This part of the peninsula – the heel of Italy's boot – has been hosting various civilizations for centuries. It was Greek, and then it was Roman; it was part of the Byzantine Empire and Norman Sicily. During the Middle Ages, Puglia was the departure point for the Crusades. The natural harbour of Brindisi hosted the ships that would eventually sail for Jerusalem, and therefore Puglia played an important role in the battle for the Holy Land. Subsequently it slipped into relative obscurity, and until recently many people – Italians included – would have associated the area only with its produce: splendid tomatoes, artichokes, mushrooms and olives from farms distinguished by fortified whitewashed farmhouses known as *masserie*.

Cheap, direct flights to Bari and Brindisi changed all that. Travellers looking for an unspoilt Italy found just that, and tourism to Puglia has increased to the point that locals have started calling Salento, the popular area south of Brindisi, 'Salentoshire'. Mercifully, despite its newly gained popularity, Puglia has changed surprisingly little. Many *masserie* have been converted into hotels, but there is no sign of the kind of rampant high-rise coastal development that has ruined many once idyllic destinations. Puglia's authentic, slow-paced charm remains intact.

In Puglia, there is no 'cultural imperative', no list of must-see landmarks to tick off. No one will notice if you don't see a single cathedral. No one will care. Puglia is about sitting in the sun, driving to the beach for a swim, heading into town for lunch and practising your *passeggiata* skills. Of course, you can stop at a cathedral if you really want to, but then it's time for another swim, followed by a siesta. In the evening you might opt for a 'fancy dinner' in the famous seaside Grotta Palazzese at Polignano a Mare or decide, instead, for a pizza in the whitewashed alleys of Locorotondo. Puglia is a place that is anti-agenda and anti-masterplan. Winging it, improvising on a daily basis, is the best way to enjoy this unpretentious stretch of Italy. And since Puglia is not that big, it is possible, with a car, to see it all...or not!

MASSERIA ALCHIMIA

A Typical Puglian Farmhouse with a Modern Touch

History, style, affordability – it's all here, a stone's throw from the sea. Alchimia combines the monumental beauty of a *masseria* with a surprisingly modern and stylish interior that won't break the bank. I love this place, not only because it's been done with such elegant taste (and restraint), but also because Alchimia is so perfectly in step with how you should experience Puglia.

Caroline, the owner and designer of this gem, knows Puglia very well, having lived here half her life. Originally from Switzerland, she was probably one of the first foreigners to succumb to the charms of a *trullo* and she used her substantial design skills to transform her dry-stone hut into a very rentable 'des res' – so much so that some regular clients who would stay at her house in the historic town of Alberobello eventually persuaded her to sell it to them. With the proceeds she purchased a whitewashed *masseria* near the coast, complete with red soil and a centuries-old olive grove, with massive, gnarly olive trees that are older than the oldest buildings in Puglia's historic towns. Thankfully,

although Caroline runs Alchimia as a hotel, she didn't parcel the handsome farmhouse into lots of small box-like rooms. Instead, it was divided into a handful of apartments that keep to the original architecture; they all have their own personality, their own kitchenettes, their own bathrooms, and private terraces or gardens.

What she created, in fact, is a paradise for independent travellers. You get the style, the space, the freedom and the privacy of an apartment without any of the headaches that usually come with renting a villa, such as fridges and pool filters not working, and having to commit many months in advance.

Alchimia is the perfect base from which to set out on your various Puglia adventures or to curl up under a twisted olive tree and immerse yourself in a book. This is not Tuscany, where you almost feel obliged to look at famous monuments. It's more like Greece, somewhere you can simply please yourself. And in the case of this *masseria*, you will be doing so with total independence and in great style.

THE *TRULLI* OF ALBEROBELLO

From a distance, *trulli* look like Smurf houses dotted throughout the Itria Valley. You cannot miss them with their distinctive painted graphics and long, cone-shaped roofs, topped by a stone cap in the shape of a ball, a cone or a disc. There is something exotic, almost pagan about them – a strange leftover, perhaps, from a lost Bronze Age civilization? They certainly set the imagination racing, but the truth is, alas, far more prosaic than you might be led to believe. Thought to date from the 16th century, these dry-stone huts were originally constructed as temporary field shelters and storehouses. The dry-stone construction, meaning that no mortar or cement was used, was an early form of tax avoidance; in theory, a *trullo* could be deconstructed in the event of a taxman's visit. What you were then supposed to do with the hundreds of stones left lying around is a bit of a puzzle. Perhaps they were hastily buried with the grain that had been stored in them. The things we do for money!

But what about the unusual stone caps that sit on top of the cone-shaped roofs? They are symbols, clearly, but of what? The answer, once again, is remarkably straightforward. A *trullisto*, a stonemason specializing in the building of *trulli*

(yes, there really was such a thing), would finish his work with a pinnacle carved from sandstone – a disc, a ball, a cone, a polyhedron, etc. – as a signature of his work.

Despite the fact that they were not placed here by aliens in prehistoric times, *trulli* are still distinctive enough to warrant getting your camera out. They may only be 400 years old – which, by Italian standards, is nothing – but they are tantalizingly photogenic. You can always make up a story to go with the picture. Who is going to fact-check a *trullo*?

One place in the Itria Valley has more *trulli* than anywhere else. In fact, Alberobello (meaning 'beautiful tree') is the only town in the whole of Italy where people live in these unusual structures, and as you might imagine, it has acquired Unesco World Heritage status because they are so rare. There's even a hotel in the town that is made up of individual *trulli*. It's sweet and it has charm, but it's not authentic. These *trulli* were built specifically for tourists, so, in a sense, it's the Alberobello version of the Wigwam Motel on Route 66 in Arizona. I'm not sure I would stay in the hotel again, but the town itself is definitely worth a visit.

MASSERIA PROSPERI

A Farm that Kept the Animals

There's no shortage of converted *masserie* in Puglia, but many have lost the connection with their farming roots in the process. Not so for super stylish Masseria Prosperi, situated north of Otranto. Goats, ducks, donkeys and even cows wander through the property at will. It's crazy and fun, and the owner Mercedes knows all the best places to share with you in the area. I would never have known about the crystal-clear turquoise waters of Baia di Marina Serra or the pale perfection of Frassanito Beach without her.

One of the problems with travel is that so often we are insulated from locals and from having a genuinely authentic experience. There is no interaction other than the odd suggestion made by a concierge, which is sad. A place like Prosperi is different because from the moment you walk through the door you are part of the community. You eat together at the same table, you learn the names of the various animals, and you meet the family and friends of the owners. Prosperi will spoil you with its food and distinct style, but it will also give you something much more precious: memories you will cherish forever.

Prosperi is an extension of the owner's love of animals, and of everything she holds dear about Puglia, but in embracing the region's farming heritage it is also a wonderfully appropriate place to stay. You can even bring your own animals if you want. There's a refreshing originality and warmth at play here. It is not short on creature comforts – there are two swimming pools, and beautiful guest suites that reflect the owner's background in fashion and design – but it is the element of fun that really makes the experience, especially if you love animals.

South of Otranto is the Masseria Montelauro, which Mercedes also runs with her family. Before moving to Puglia, she lived in Milan and worked in fashion, as did her mother. One year she convinced her mother to holiday in Puglia, instead of the usual Portofino or Sardinia. They fell for Puglia's earthy, authentic charm in such a big way that they decided to buy a *masseria*. It was far too big to be a holiday home, and before anyone knew it the family was in the hotel business with their newly revamped Masseria Montelauro. They kept it simple and applied their natural style to everything from the whitewashed interiors to the presentation of the food. The vaulted ceilings and huge whitewashed walls that were part of the original structure were retained. A pool was added in the courtyard, and a pergola was constructed over a space where they serve breakfast. Simple good taste is the secret of Montelauro's success.

BURY YOUR TOES IN THE SAND

For centuries, this picturesque stretch of Adriatic coast faced the near-constant threat of invasion due to its strategic location, its length and its fertile farmland. It was colonized by both the ancient Greeks and the Romans, and later became part of the Byzantine Empire, whose influence can still be felt today in churches such as Chiesa di San Pietro in Otranto, which is believed to date from the 10th century. During the Crusades, the coast of Puglia was also the preferred departure point for Christian knights bound for Jerusalem, with ships setting sail from the natural harbour of Brindisi.

Historically Puglia has been invaded by just about every major power of the day, but now it is experiencing an invasion of a different kind: by sun-seeking tourists from all over Europe. There are

worse places to invade! The food is brilliant, and so is the weather, but the one thing Puglia does not have is an abundance of beaches. Granted, the sea is a wonderful turquoise colour, especially south of Brindisi, but most of the coastline is formed of craggy cliffs. Even when you come across the odd inlet along the coast, they rarely have a crescent of sand. That's what makes the beach just north of Otranto so exceptional. It is fine, pale and powdery, broad and long, with real dunes, like a beach in Australia or Brazil. Strangely, or perhaps luckily, most Italian beach-goers seem to gravitate towards the section of this beach that has the daybeds, the umbrellas, the snack bars...and the noise.

If you are like me and prefer beaches that are empty and pristine, head left. But be warned, the local parking police can be tricky, and that's a polite way of putting it! I am still getting traffic infringement notices and hefty fines for what amounts to parking under a tree next to a beach in the middle of nowhere. The best way, by far, to bury your toes here and avoid any dread about what might be arriving in the mail afterwards is to stay at the beautiful and wonderfully authentic Masseria Prosperi, situated just across the road. From this working farm that has, thankfully, kept its animals and its rustic charm, it is no more than a three-minute walk to what must surely be the best beach in Puglia.

CONVENTO DI SANTA MARIA DI COSTANTINOPOLI

15th-century Convent Filled with Tribal Art

This former Franciscan monastery is situated as far southeast as you can go in Italy, on the tip of the heel of the boot. It's exactly the kind of property I would have expected Alistair McAlpine to find, with his intuitive sense for the exotic and remote. I first met him when he was nearing completion on his Cable Beach project in Broome, Western Australia – the result of a classic Alistair McAlpine moment of inspired spontaneity. Years before, his plane had landed at Broome en route to Darwin from Perth. Intrigued by this pearling town in the middle of nowhere, he got off and by the time he boarded the plane again he had purchased Broome's prime beachfront – named Cable Beach because it marked the point where the telegraph cables from Indonesia first landed on Australian shores. He ended up building a resort there, furnishing it with priceless antiques from India and populating it with exotic wild animals from Africa, which ran around the garden (seriously).

Most people knew him as Lord McAlpine of West Green, Margaret Thatcher's Tory treasurer and scion of the well-known McAlpine family that made its fortune in engineering and construction; I knew him as a passionate collector and someone who never failed to follow his instinct for exotic beauty. I remember when a friend made a remarkable chair from animal bones that he had found on his family's property, a remote station in the Northern Territory. Not only did Alistair buy it, but he also commissioned my friend to cast the 'bone' chair in bronze for the dining room of his palazzo in Venice. Sadly, Alistair is no longer around but his extraordinary 'eye' survives in the convent that he and his wife, Athena, rescued in the south of Salento.

When Alistair and Athena first found the Convento di Santa Maria di Costantinopoli, the owner had been using it to keep his animals; he had won the property in a card game, so it had little sentimental value. At first the McAlpines were simply looking for a place to settle, but as restoration work progressed they decided it would be more fun to make some of the rooms available to friends and family. Out of this grew what must surely rank as one of the most extraordinary overnight experiences in all of Italy – like sleeping in a museum, although much more luxurious and comfortable. Collections of textiles, African furniture, figurines, tribal artefacts and books – about 14,000 of them – line the corridors and decorate every nook and cranny.

What's most surprising, perhaps, is how relaxed Lady McAlpine is with the presence of guests among so many priceless pieces. They are part of the experience, nothing more – no fuss is made, and that's how it should be.

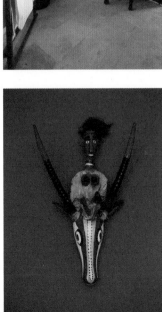

JUMP
FROM THE
CLIFFS OF
LO SCALO

Two questions seem to crop up in almost every travel scenario: 'What are we doing today?' and 'Where are we having lunch?' In the south of Puglia, where the Adriatic meets the Ionian Sea, there's a place that deals with both questions simultaneously.

Follow a small road that winds its way down the Salento coast from the town of Marittima di Diso, where the Convento di Santa Maria di Costantinopoli is located. Eventually you arrive at a sign and a left-hand turn for Marina di Novaglie, which takes you down an unpaved road to Lo Scalo, an unexpectedly chic restaurant situated in one of the most beautiful locations in Puglia. The restaurant is not much more than an open platform, protected by a lightweight canopy, but it is perched on the edge of a rocky cliff blessed with a panoramic view of the most turquoise sea imaginable; just a bunch of chairs and tables in the middle of nowhere with a knockout view, but Italy being Italy, the tables are immaculately set with linen and the waiters turn out in spotless attire.

Lo Scalo obviously has a reputation for its food because, despite being in the middle of nowhere, it was full. The menu, not surprisingly, features a lot of Italian seafood dishes, and there is live entertainment (don't worry, no one crooning 'Volare') in the form of local cliff diving. While you are waiting for your food to arrive, you will see people jumping from the rocky outcrops that surround the restaurant, into the crystal-clear waters below. My kids couldn't wait for lunch to finish so that they could do the same.

As long as you have a swimsuit and a pair of trainers that you don't mind getting wet (so you don't cut your feet on the sharp rocks), you really don't need much else. The trick with the jumping is to start low and work your way up to the higher spots on the cliff. With practice comes courage. The most practical advice is to follow the example of the locals, who know where to jump.

That's what we did. All afternoon, after lunch, we literally jumped for joy!

ROME

AND

LAZIO

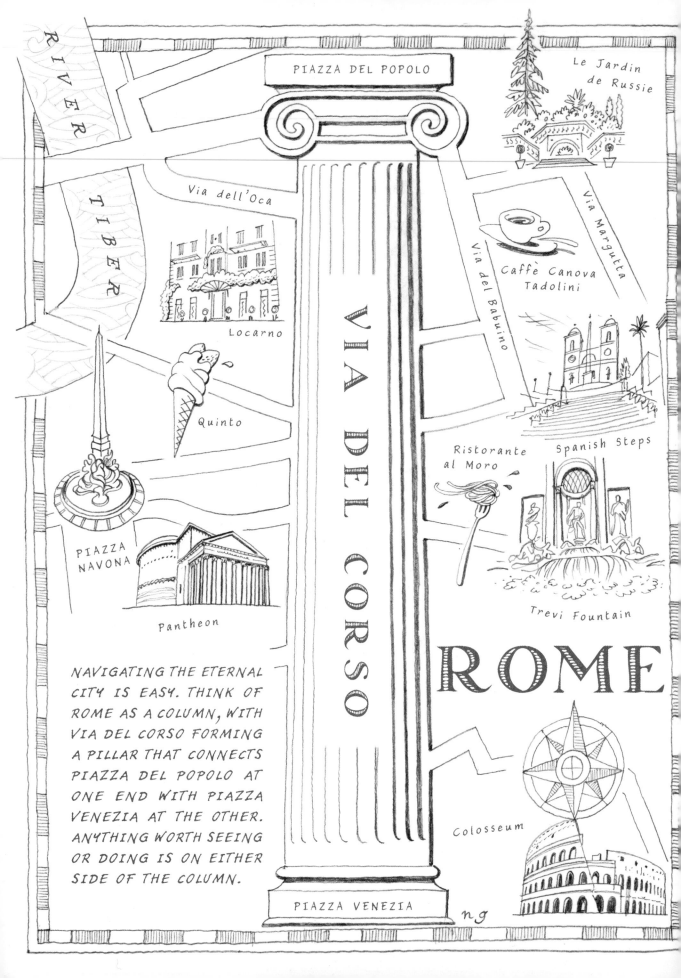

RIVER

TIBER

PIAZZA DEL POPOLO

Le Jardin de Russie

Via dell'Oca

Via Margutta

Via del Babuino

Caffè Canova Tadolini

Locarno

Quinto

Spanish Steps

Ristorante al Moro

PIAZZA NAVONA

Pantheon

Trevi Fountain

VIA DEL CORSO

ROME

NAVIGATING THE ETERNAL CITY IS EASY. THINK OF ROME AS A COLUMN, WITH VIA DEL CORSO FORMING A PILLAR THAT CONNECTS PIAZZA DEL POPOLO AT ONE END WITH PIAZZA VENEZIA AT THE OTHER. ANYTHING WORTH SEEING OR DOING IS ON EITHER SIDE OF THE COLUMN.

Colosseum

PIAZZA VENEZIA

ng

Do As Romans Do
– Eat!

Rome is the Eternal City – we all know that. Nowhere else on earth has had so much history, for so long. Perhaps that's why so many visitors act as if they are on a school trip, standing in line for hours at the Vatican, shuffling dutifully from monument to monument, ticking off the sights from a never-ending list. It is as if they have an obligation to see it all and must write an essay at the end of the trip that they will be marked on. That's not the 'sweet life', and ironically it's not very Roman either.

When Rome was the world's largest metropolis, the first city with sewers and aqueducts and other amenities that made life more bearable and structured, it wasn't celebrated for these public conveniences. It was famous for its taverns, theatres and brothels, and for sports arenas that showcased unimaginably gory spectacles in noisy, massive (even by today's standards) stadiums. Rome was a hedonists' dream, and that's why everyone wanted to visit it. Centuries later, Catholic Rome may have toned it down a bit, but do you honestly think people came here from all over the world only to pray?

Enjoying life is what Romans do, as they have done for an eternity. So go ahead and be historically correct: have some fun in Rome. By no means am I suggesting you ignore the pearls of an unparalleled history – far from it! I just think you can do both. How better to appreciate Borghese's Gardens than to have lunch in them? How better to soak up the atmosphere of the Pantheon than to have it all to yourself at breakfast? And how better to understand the genius of Canova than to have a cappuccino in his former home and studio?

BREAKFAST AT THE PANTHEON

Escape the Crowds

The Pantheon is a 2,000-year-old marvel of engineering. It takes your breath away to think that this masterpiece, completed by Emperor Hadrian around AD 125 and originally dedicated to the pagan gods of Rome, has stood in the same spot for nearly two millennia. More remarkable is the fact that its massive dome, which has a hole in the apex and opens to the sky, was made from moulded concrete lozenges set into a wooden frame; it remains the largest unreinforced concrete dome in the world. Who knew that concrete even existed in ancient Rome?

Visitors through the centuries have been dumbfounded by the innovative construction and precise geometry of this extraordinary temple. When Filippo Brunelleschi, for instance, was trying to work out how to build the dome of Florence's famous cathedral, he looked to the Pantheon for clues. And then there are those enormous granite columns: the soaring monoliths that would be difficult to quarry today, even with all the modern technology available. To think how this was done (not to mention how they were transported), in an age without mechanical cranes and hydraulic machinery, defies the imagination. The Pantheon is, without doubt, the most exceptional survivor from ancient Rome,

and if you visit nothing else in the city, you must see this.

Regrettably, the crowds can tarnish the experience. The Pantheon requires silence – an atmosphere of contemplation – if it is to be appreciated fully; it was a temple after all, and is now a church. During the day, especially in the warmer months, silence is simply not an option. The gravitas of this historic gem is completely drowned out by horse-drawn carriages touting for business, by street vendors trying to sell you things, and by flag-bearing tour guides yelling at their exhausted, camera-laden flocks.

To experience the Pantheon properly, you need to get up early and leave your hotel by 7 a.m. Make sure your route takes you through Piazza di Pietra, past the imposing fluted columns of the Temple of Hadrian; keep walking, with the columns on your left, and you will soon get to the next square, Piazza della Rotonda, home to the Pantheon. Now grab a table at Scusate Il Ritardo (meaning 'sorry to keep you waiting'), right next to the Pantheon, and order your cappuccino and a Nutella-filled *cornetto*. Take your time to bask in the beauty of this ancient place of worship and absorb the extraordinary sense of history – there's no better way to see it.

PIAZZA NAVONA STANDS OUT FROM OTHER PIAZZAS

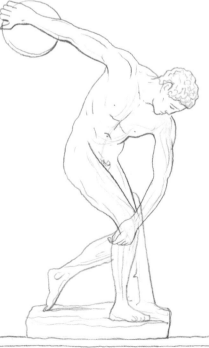

THE ROMANS WEREN'T JUST BUSY CONQUERING THE WORLD. THEY WERE ALSO BUSY BRINGING BITS OF IT BACK TO ROME, ESPECIALLY OBELISKS. RENAISSANCE

POPES WERE ALSO FOND OF THESE EGYPTIAN SOUVENIRS.
BUT HOW COULD CATHOLIC ROME JUSTIFY PAGAN
MONUMENTS? EASY – PUT A CROSS ON IT!

FOUR RIVERS

The Most Beautiful Fountain in Rome

Of all the fountains in Rome, the most poetic, the most artistic, the most original and surely the most beautiful is Gian Lorenzo Bernini's Fontana dei Quattro Fiumi (Fountain of the Four Rivers) – completed in 1651 – in Piazza Navona. Pope Innocent X commissioned it after launching a design competition for a fountain for the square, which is also home to the imposing church of Sant'Agnese in Agone, of which his wealthy family were patrons. Due to politics Bernini, the master of the baroque, was curiously *not* invited to take part, but friends urged him to make a maquette of his design; they then, surreptitiously, arranged for it to be placed in the Pope's family palace – Palazzo Pamphili on Piazza Navona – in a spot where he would see it. The sneaky strategy paid off. When Innocent X saw the model, it is said he was brought to tears...as was the competition. How could he not commission Bernini's masterpiece? 'God', he argued, 'would never forgive him.'

Intended as a celebration of the global reach of the Catholic Church, the fountain depicts four rivers representing the four continents known to man at the time: the Ganges for Asia, the Danube for Europe, Río de la Plata for the Americas, and the Nile for Africa. From a circular basin, mountainous rocks – sculpted from travertine marble – rise to support four river gods languishing among cascades that spill and splash into rock pools and grottoes populated by lions, horses and crocodiles. Some of the heroic figures look up in awe at an ancient Egyptian obelisk rising above them, made by order of the emperor Domitian in the 1st century AD. This base is surmounted by the Pamphili family emblem, which features a dove holding an olive branch.

Bernini's masterpiece is packed with exquisite detail, such as the pile of silver coins on which the Río de la Plata god sits, symbolizing the potential wealth of this unexplored continent, and the oar of the Ganges figure, reflecting the fact that the river is navigable. But, for me, the detail that takes this sculpture into the 'genius' category is the crumpled piece of linen – carved from white marble, no less – draped over the eyes of the Nile god. His eyes are cloaked because, at the time, the source of the Nile was unknown.

OBELISKS

A Roman Obsession

More obelisks stand in Rome than in any other place in the world – Egypt included. The ancient Romans were so obsessed with them that they built special 'obelisk ships', designed for no other purpose than to transport these megaliths – which could reach over 30 m in length and weigh more than 400 metric tons – up the Nile and across the Mediterranean. And when they started running out of obelisks from temples along the Nile, they commissioned them from scratch. Of the thirteen obelisks that currently stand in the Eternal City, eight are authentic and five are Roman – made in Egypt, to order.

A monumental amount of money, time and effort was invested in these gargantuan blocks of stone, although for the eight real ones in particular it was warranted because they were extraordinary antiques. The Flaminio Obelisk, for instance, in Piazza del Popolo, was made for Ramses II in the 13th century BC. When the Roman emperor Augustus first laid eyes on this 24-m giant in the Temple of the Sun in Heliopolis, he was looking at a monument that was 1,300 years old. In anybody's book, that rates as a significant souvenir.

Strangely enough, most of the obelisks that were dragged to Rome disappeared with the fall of the Roman Empire in the 5th century AD; not stolen, but buried. It's difficult to imagine how one might lose such an enormous monument, and equally hard to consider how much earth or rubble would be needed to do so; but disappear they did, for around a thousand years. All except one, that is: the Vatican Obelisk, which stands at the centre of St Peter's Square and bears no hieroglyphics, has the distinction of never having toppled during its 2,000-year tenure in Rome. I'm sure the symbolism of this was not lost on the Vatican, and it may even have been the reason why the obelisk was moved during the Renaissance from a side position to a dominantly central one. Many of the remaining obelisks were found in the late 1500s, purely by accident, as a result of new building works by the Catholic Church. So, just to put that into a very Roman perspective (with their love of irony): these massive pagan monuments resurfaced as a direct result of the expansion plans of the Catholic Church. Even Dan Brown could not have scripted such a tantalizingly ironic twist.

Better still, the person in charge of new building projects was Pope Sixtus V, and it was the Pope, and subsequent popes after him, who ordered the excavation and resurrection of these extraordinary monuments. In today's political world, they probably would have been buried again, only deeper! But the popes of Renaissance Rome were highly educated sophisticates from wealthy families that cared deeply for history and art and beauty in all disciplines, even pagan ones.

LE JARDIN DE RUSSIE

Lunch in a Secret Garden

After the fall of the Roman Empire, the Catholic Church was responsible for much of Rome's beautification. Wealthy cardinals and powerful popes commissioned handsome buildings and splendid monuments, and some also invested in spectacular gardens. The greenest fingers of all belonged to Cardinal Scipione Borghese, who in the early 17th century spent vast sums on turning his former vineyard into the most extensive garden complex to be conceived in Rome since antiquity. As a nephew of Pope Paul V and a patron of Bernini, Cardinal Borghese had the connections and taste to introduce exquisite fountains, statues, trees, lakes and temples into his vast estate. He had a talent that was characteristic of Renaissance Italy of being able to 'enhance' the beauty of nature. His legacy survives today in the Borghese Gardens, a splendid public park of 80 hectares that functions as the lungs of Rome, at the top of the Pincian Hill.

What is not commonly known, however, is that a small part of Borghese's original gardens still exists as a *giardino segreto*, or secret garden. Completely obscured from public view by the grand façade of Hotel de Russie on Via del Babuino, the garden creates a remarkable backdrop for one of Rome's best restaurants, Le Jardin de Russie. It is a world within a world. While the rest of Rome is noisy, bustling and hot, this secret garden is cool and serene. The terraces that define the garden – complete with fountains, stone steps, marble balustrades and lush greenery that cascades from one level to the next – are chiselled into the steep face of the Pincian Hill, enveloping the diner in what amounts to a monumental green space.

The food matches the surroundings. Between April and November, I cannot think of a more beautiful and enchanting place to eat. Try the octopus and cuttlefish *alla cacciatora*, or pici pasta with shrimps and pistachios, and be sure to have the fig tart with Brachetto for dessert. If you have lunch only once in Rome, make sure it's here.

HAVE COFFEE WITH CANOVA

By the early 19th century, the Venetian-born, Rome-based sculptor Antonio Canova was the most acclaimed artist in Europe and had some of the biggest clients on the Continent, including Pope Pius VII and Napoleon. His adventures in the upper echelons of power and privilege generated some fabulous stories, particularly concerning the work he did for Napoleon and

his family. Canova was initially commissioned to make a bust of Napoleon in 1802, which led to discussions about a full statue. Napoleon wanted to be depicted in a French general's uniform but Canova, cleverly manipulating Napoleon's narcissistic side, convinced him that he should appear as Mars, the Roman God of War. And so a larger-than-life marble statue

was made, ironically titled *Napoleon as Mars the Peacemaker*. The statue arrived in Paris in 1811, when Napoleon was still in power, but it was never installed. After Napoleon's defeat at the Battle of Waterloo in 1815, the British government purchased the statue and presented it to the victorious Duke of Wellington, who placed it in the stairwell of his stately home, Apsley House in London, where it stands to this day. There's a wonderful, almost poetic irony to the fact that the military commander who finally put Napoleon in his place should have a giant, naked sculpture of his nemesis at the bottom of his stairs. They just don't make revenge as stylish as this anymore.

Canova went on to make many more masterpieces and today his work is spread, quite democratically, among the world's most prestigious museums. But perhaps his most notorious piece stands in the smallest venue: the exquisite Galleria Borghese in Rome. Completed in 1808, *Venus Victrix* is a semi-nude sculpture of Pauline Bonaparte, the sister of Napoleon, when the emperor was still in power. Canova had imagined her as Diana, suitably dressed in ancient Roman attire, but Pauline (who was a Borghese by marriage) was having none of it. She insisted that the statue be nude, because, as she explained to Canova, it was not intended for display. She wanted to be Venus, not Diana. Canova was quite a handsome rogue and Pauline had a certain reputation, so the mind boggles at what went on during all those months of 'posing'... (An appointment is required to visit the Galleria Borghese; if you are staying in a hotel, they should be able to arrange it for you.)

So, now you have some background, you can begin to understand how weird and wonderful it is that Canova's former home and studio at 150a Via del Babuino presently operates as a café. At Caffè Canova Tadolini you are surrounded by the neoclassical master's myriad plaster maquettes and studies – the words 'embarrassment of riches' come to mind! Only in Rome do you find a place like this, where you can have Canova with your pastry and cappuccino.

DISCOVER THE ARTISTS' STREET

Every year, Rome hosts an art festival called 'One Hundred Painters of Via Margutta', a unique occasion when a thousand or more works of art line the shaded cobblestones of this picturesque little street. Although it is not far from the Spanish Steps and is thoroughly connected to the arts, Via Margutta has somehow managed to retain its authenticity, but do not imagine that it is unimportant. Via Margutta has quite a pedigree! This is where the city's first dedicated artists' studios were built. In fact, when Picasso was briefly resident in Rome in 1917, he kept such a studio at 53B Via Margutta; here, he worked on costumes and sets for Diaghilev's Ballets Russes, as well as painting his newly found love interest, the Russian ballerina Olga Khokhlova.

A decade later, in quintessentially Roman fashion, a fountain designed by Pietro Lombardi was dedicated to the street's artists. The Fontana degli Artisti is a travertine fountain crowned by a bucket of paint brushes, and features two masks facing in opposite directions – one happy, one sad – that represent the fluctuating moods of an artist. On a hot day, many passers-by, especially locals, stop to drink from the fountain.

Situated at the base of the Pincian Hill, Via Margutta was once a street of craftsmen and stonemasons. It was the kind of environment that attracted artists from all over Italy and beyond. Over a period of several hundred years it evolved from a back street of workshops into a bohemian enclave and, finally, a beacon for directors and writers, as well as painters. Legendary filmmaker Federico Fellini – director of *La Dolce Vita* – lived and worked here, as did the talented painter Renato Guttuso and the author Marina Ripa di Meana. For a brief time during the 1950s, this part of Rome became the cultural centre of the world – a story well documented by Giampiero Mughini in his book *Che Belle le Ragazze di Via Margutta* (2004).

But arguably the most famous moment in the history of this narrow, leafy street was when Gregory Peck and Audrey Hepburn arrived in the back of a cab at 51 Via Margutta, the address of ex-pat journalist Joe Bradley, whom Peck portrayed in the 1953 film *Roman Holiday*. The movie made both Hepburn and the Vespa scooter a household name, and she received an Academy Award for her portrayal of Ann, the reluctant and bored princess who wanted some excitement in her life.

Remarkably, despite all this attention, Via Margutta has not changed much – it still has that artists' vibe. Compared to the rest of Rome, this long and narrow lane is quiet and peaceful and attractively green. There are a couple of restaurants, a few highly original antique emporiums, a workshop making gilded frames, a gallery selling busts from Roman antiquity, and a showroom for Rubelli fabrics, but little else goes on, and that's exactly the way everyone likes it.

IT IS KNOWN AS THE TRIDENT, NAMED AFTER NEPTUNE'S WEAPON —

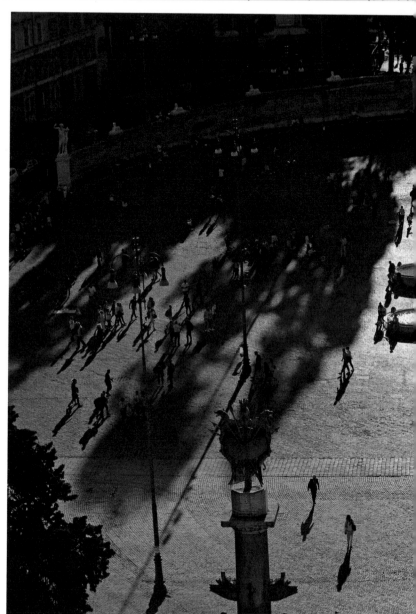

 THE THREE PRONGS OF THE TRIDENT ARE VIA

ST RESTAURANTS, BARS, BOUTIQUES AND CAFÉS.

PETTA, VIA DEL CORSO AND VIA DEL BABUINO,

EXTENDING FROM PIAZZA DEL POPOLO AT THE BASE OF THE SHAFT.

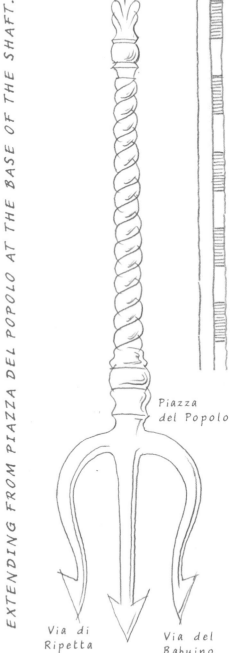

Piazza
del Popolo

Via di
Ripetta

Via del
Corso

Via del
Babuino

LOCARNO

A Legend is Born

Ever since the graphic artist Anselmo Ballester created the award-winning Hotel Locarno poster in 1925, this unassuming address, around the corner from Piazza del Popolo, has become more and more of a legend. It was a lot smaller when I first checked in two decades ago, but the crowd was the same: a bohemian mix of film directors, authors, architects, artists and designers. The place had an arty vibe that attracted an enviably cool clientele; it still does.

The list of famous guests may be long and steady, but refreshingly this was never the aim. Maria Teresa Celli, the owner, proved that not so long ago when she refused Woody Allen's request to use the hotel as a location for his 2012 film *To Rome With Love*. 'Why would we do that?' she exclaimed. 'All that nonsense, just for a film.' And that was that. Goodbye, Woody! That's why I love this place. It has character, and it doesn't try too hard.

Although the hotel's history dates back to the 1920s, when a Swiss couple set up the nostalgically named Albergo Locarno, the real Locarno – the legend – was started by accident in the 1970s. Celli had an appointment to see a building on Via dell'Oca but the agent was running late. She decided to use the time to look at the property across the road. By the time the agent had turned up, Celli was embarking on

a new life. She had decided to create a hotel – a place that would recall the spirit and style of the Belle Epoque. Her daughter, Caterina Valente (who now runs the hotel), remembers all too well the endless visits to flea markets with her mother to find genuine Art Deco and Art Nouveau pieces. Point to any object in the hotel and Caterina will tell you the story: of how, for instance, the Tiffany lamp on the bar came from Buenos Aires, and how as a child she cradled it in her lap on the flight home with her mother; or how they scoured flea markets all over Italy to find enough chairs of the same style for the bar and the restaurant.

Then, a number of years ago, an opportunity arose to buy the building next door. It had been built by a Venetian family in 1905, and had floors of polished terrazzo and marble bathrooms. The rooms were also much larger, with higher ceilings, adding some 'grand style' to the cool vibe. The outdoor space between the two buildings lent itself perfectly for conversion to a courtyard, which has since become one of the hottest (or coolest?) cocktail bars in Rome.

One thing you can rely on with Caterina and her mother is that they will never rest on their laurels. As Caterina will tell you, they keep working at one simple goal: to make Locarno the kind of place where they would want to stay.

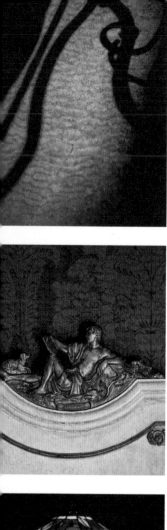

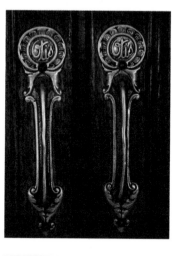

VIA DELL'OCA

A Mini Margutta in the Making

Via dell' Oca, just around the corner from Piazza del Popolo, shares the same sense of authenticity and effortless style of nearby Via Margutta. It's a tiny street, but this short stretch of real estate houses more unique boutiques than the entire length of 'touristy' Via del Corso – and it's no accident. Fed up with the endless onslaught of what she refers to as 'plastic ham' establishments in her native city, Caterina Valente, the driving force behind Hotel Locarno, decided to do something about it. Every time a lease expired on a shop on Via dell'Oca, across the street from her hotel, she took it. She had no idea what she was going to do with it, but one thing she did know: it was not going to be a T-shirt and postcard shop or worse – yet another pizzeria with a fake ham in the window. Over her dead body!

The solution for what to do with her growing collection of empty shops came the way that best things often do – by word of mouth. People heard about it – creative people who admire what she and her mother started with Hotel Locarno, people who understand the commercial potential of being unique and are drawn by the same set of values and convictions.

That's how this 'mini Margutta' ended up with Artisanal Cornucopia, Elif Sallorenzo's collection of oriental treasures ranging from beaded 'Capri-esque' sandals to dinner plates painted with dashing portraits of sultans in extravagant turbans. That's also how 'the street across the street' got an Eau D'Italie Le Sirenuse Positano boutique – a small, super-smart modern-day 'apothecary' specializing in the 'scents of Italy'. It's wonderful to know that there is nowhere else on the planet where you can buy these uniquely packaged essences of Italy (unless you happen to be a guest at Le Sirenuse, that is). Then there is Cristina Bomba, a designer/tailor with a fashion shop that makes beautiful ties, scarves and dresses. Next door is the only Roman outlet for Italian couturier Laura Urbinati, another shop filled with original pieces. But perhaps the best story is Patrizia Fabri's. This legendary milliner's boutique got started only because Fabri had heard about Rome's pre-eminent milliner – Signor Cirri and his plans to retire – which left the question: What to do with the thousands of hand-carved wooden lasts that he still had in his workshop? She couldn't bear the idea of these extraordinary examples of handcraft being ignored or, worse, destroyed, so she bought the lot and became a milliner. No business plan, no opening party, just a determination to do something that seemed eminently worth doing.

HUNT DOWN THE BEST HOMEMADE *GELATI* IN ROME

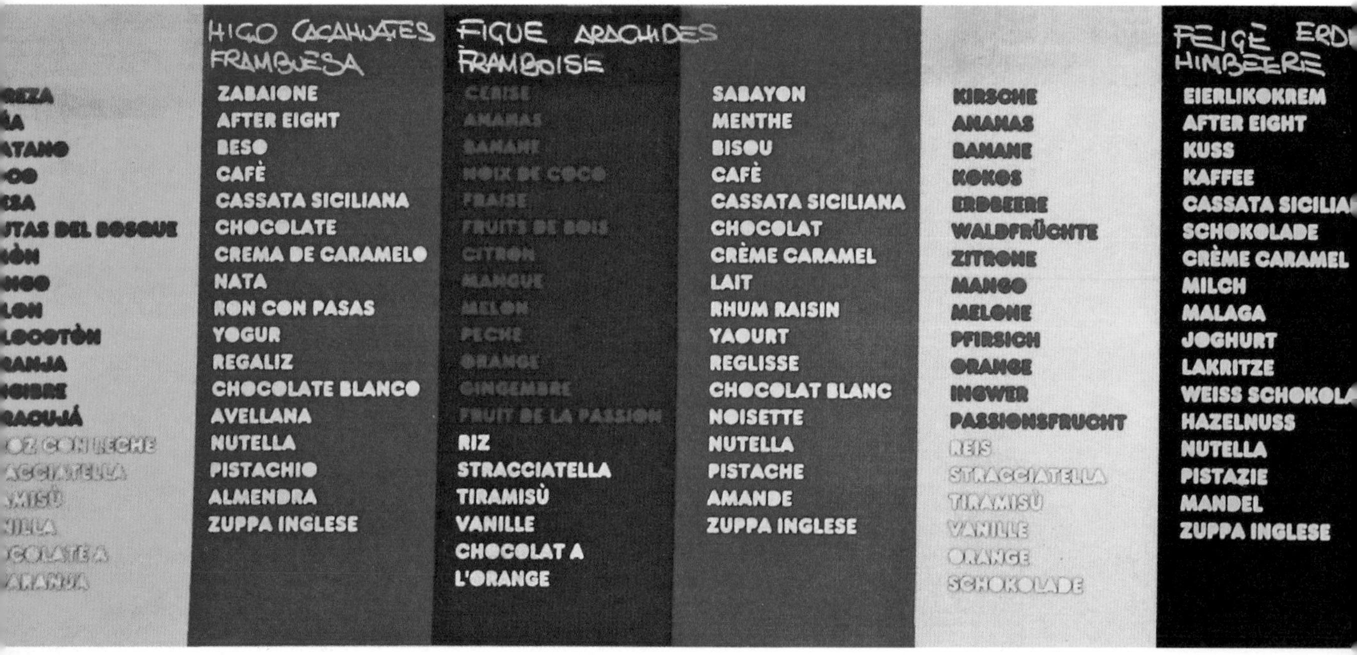

There is certainly no shortage of *gelaterie* in Rome, but how can you be certain that the ice cream you are holding was made by hand with fresh ingredients? Of course, there are some simple warning signs: a fluffy whipped appearance in the display tubs, although visually attractive, usually means chemical stiffeners have been added, and an unusually bright flavour is a dead giveaway for artificial colourings. But the short answer is: you can't know for sure.

To find the real thing, you need to ask one question: where do the locals go? The answer is Quinto, on Via di Tor Millina, not far from Piazza Navona, which has been serving homemade ice cream from the same shop for a hundred years. It's a family business that features more than a hundred flavours, all homemade and handmade. The shop is decorated like a refrigerator door – a riot of postcards, pictures, menus, straws, paper cups and handmade signs – but Romans come here for the *gelati*, not the decor. When you talk to the family behind the counter about their *gelati*, their eyes light up. They have a passion for what they do that has passed from one generation to the next and is as strong now as it has ever been.

TRATTORIA AL MORO

Roman Cuisine a Coin's Throw from the Trevi Fountain

I am not a big fan of the Trevi Fountain. Even before it was renovated, this baroque fantasy was so ridiculously overcrowded that tourists were practically waiting in line to toss their coins. It's a far cry from the deserted, quietly romantic monument visited by Gregory Peck and Audrey Hepburn in *Roman Holiday*, and even further from the iconic scene in *La Dolce Vita*. To imagine the voluptuous Anita Ekberg, today, scandalously wading into the fountain in her low-cut black cocktail dress is simply impossible. With the amount of security surrounding the site, she would be arrested before she even got a toe in the water.

And now that the Trevi Fountain has been scrubbed perfectly clean, I find it even less appealing. Having said all that, I do understand that it's probably down as a must-see if you're on a trip of a lifetime to Rome, so I have a suggestion. Go in the evening, after your *aperitivo*. Drop a few coins in the fountain (make sure you use your left hand and take comfort from the fact that all the coins go to Caritas, a Catholic relief organization). Take the mandatory 'selfie' (if you must) and then go for dinner, as a reward for persevering, in an extraordinary restaurant

close by that tourists will never find because it is hiding in plain sight.

Trattoria al Moro is one of the oldest and most consistent restaurants in Rome, on an unassuming little alleyway called Vicolo delle Bollette. The front door is plain, the outside walls could do with a lick of paint and the sign is dated, but all of this is intentional. It is theatre, put on by the restaurant to discourage passers-by from entering. It may sound unkind, but the truth is Al Moro does very well on the back of its Roman clientele, and this repeat business is far more valuable than the odd tourist dropping in. Besides, it's a family business, which means the family know most of the clientele and vice versa.

This was one of Fellini's favourite haunts. He would come here, as Romans still do, for the pasta alla carbonara, the Scampi al Moro or the fettuccine with white truffles (in season in the autumn). Al Moro is virtually 'Romans only', but don't let that deter you. I went with my wife after a friend phoned ahead and booked us in, and the staff made us feel like we had been going there all our lives. The food was amazing, the wines were superb, and we were honorary Romans if only for the night.

Escape
from Rome Without
Going Far

Unless you follow Italian football, you've probably never heard of Lazio, one of twenty administrative regions in Italy, of which Rome is the capital. The countryside surrounding the Eternal City never gets much press, which suits a lot of Romans quite well. As in most cities, many people like to get out of Rome for the weekend, and you might be surprised to learn that mountains and beaches are within easy reach. An hour and a half's drive from the centre of Rome, for instance, will take you into countryside that bears a striking resemblance to the forgotten corners of Umbria or Tuscany. Forty-five minutes will get you to the beach.

The more mountainous option is certainly the more fashionable one. To be perfectly candid, most of the coast near Rome is flat, uninspiring and overdeveloped, and unless you are staying at the very glamorous Posta Vecchia, which has a black sand beach of its own, I wouldn't bother. The rolling hills of Lazio, on the other hand, especially the ones that border towns such as Orvieto, are so similar to neighbouring Umbria that it's easy to confuse the two. If you were to blindfold me and drop me into the village square of Civita di Bagnoregio, I would swear I was in Umbria. The appeal lies in the charm and authenticity of these small villages perched on hilltops in splendid landscapes. For city-dwellers it's not just a chance to breathe clean air but an opportunity to escape to a simpler life. There's not much to do but walk around, have a coffee in a village square, strike up some conversation and arrange to meet friends for lunch. All of this, of course, suits Romans very well because they love eating and talking!

CIVITA DI BAGNOREGIO

The Tumbling Town

From a distance, Civita di Bagnoregio looks like a scene from *The Lord of the Rings*: a tiny medieval town perched on a plateau, with sheer drops into deep valleys on all sides. You half expect to find Gandalf the Grey walking along the cobblestones of the steeply ascending, vertigo-inducing footbridge that crosses the ravine, which separates the town from the rest of the world. But it's not a film set: people live here, even if for some it's only for the weekend (the population is low teens in the winter and around 200 in the summer).

The isolated, exposed peak hardly looks large enough to support a town that has a piazza, a church, cafés, a bar, trattorias and a dozen or so houses; and that's not far from the truth because every once in a while a chunk breaks off and tumbles into the abyss, taking a building with it. Erosion, over time, is literally making the town smaller. Italians refer to it as *la città che muore* ('the dying town'), as described so beautifully in this passage by the writer Bonaventura Tecchi, who was born in the satellite town of Bagnoregio: 'I would never have become a writer if I had not lived for a few months every year, from July to November, starting in my earliest youth, in the valley of Civita, with the vision of the white crests, the golden volcanic clay, the eloquent ruins, in the land of Saint Bonaventure, the city that is dying...'

Civita di Bagnoregio has quite a history. It was founded by the Etruscans 2,500 years ago and was the birthplace of St Bonaventure, in the 13th century, although the house where he was born has long since disappeared off the cliff. Despite its diminutive size, Civita has played a major role for the Catholic Church almost since the beginning. There has been a bishop of Civita di Bagnoregio, for instance, since around AD 600 when Pope St Gregory the Great confirmed the appointment in writing – an appointment as diocese that continues to this day, although it has been renamed the Diocese of Viterbo. That's how such a tiny town ended up with such a large church. I've read that it even qualified as a cathedral until earthquake damage justified building a newer one in Bagnoregio in the late 1600s.

Just behind the church is the bishop's former residence, and behind that, a school for training priests that is now operated as a B&B – a place appropriately called Corte della Maestà ('Court of Majesty').

CORTE DELLA MAESTÀ

The Seductive Charm of a Converted Priests' College

Corte della Maestà is hidden away in a secluded spot behind an anonymous timber gate in the centre of Civita di Bagnoregio. The entrance is next to a garden, which is perhaps not something you would expect to find in such a tiny, precariously situated town. Once upon a time this was a school for priests, but now there's little trace of this former ascetic life. The guest spaces have been converted, beautifully, into the type of accommodation you would normally find in the pages of *Architectural Digest*. It almost seems too chic, too stylish, to be a B&B.

But it is. Corte della Maestà must rank as one of the most beautiful and exotic B&Bs in Italy, with an unprecedented location, stunning views, some impressive history and genuine celebrity credentials. It is owned by Paolo Crepet and his glamorous wife Cristiana; he is one of Italy's best-known psychiatrists with a popular show on Italian television and works in Rome during the week, and she is a former model who manages the property and created all of its splendid interiors. They live in the old bishop's house next door.

The key word for the Corte della Maestà experience is 'taste'. It has been put together with such great taste; and I don't just mean the interiors, but the guest experience as a whole. In the morning, for instance, breakfast – prepared by the immaculate Cristiana – is served in the garden, under a cast-iron rose arbour completely hidden from the outside world. During the day, being here gives you the best location from which to get out and explore the town, and surprisingly for such a small place, there are quite a few choices in terms of where to eat.

Civita is a popular destination for day tourists and usually attracts a few hundred people at a time – enough to give the town some life, but not so many that it spoils the effect. It is unlikely ever to get out of hand because all visitors must climb the steep footbridge to get here; there is no motorized traffic (except a funny little three-wheeler for the occasional bride and groom descending from the church). An added bonus, particularly in the warmer months, is that you're likely to witness a wedding. I was here for two days and saw two.

But the best part, by far, is that at the end of the day, everyone else has to go back over the bridge – back to the real world – while you get to stay here, with Gandalf.

LA POSTA VECCHIA

Renaissance Palazzo with a Black Sand Beach

For years, J. Paul Getty, once the richest man on earth, tried to convince his aristocratic friends – the Odescalchi family – to sell him their double-fronted Renaissance palazzo in Ladispoli, on the coast outside Rome. It's not hard to see what attracted Getty. This may well be the only Renaissance palazzo ever built on a beach. The name, by the way, stems from the time that the palazzo was a stop on the mail route, which would have been a prestigious role to have.

History, pedigree and *pieds dans l'eau*, La Posta Vecchia had it all – and Getty wanted it. In the end, the Odescalchis, who still own the medieval fort on the same stretch of coast (the one you can see from La Posta Vecchia's windows), gave in and the palazzo became Getty's main home. He wasted no time turning it into his own museum. With the help of several respected historians and antiquarians, he stocked the house with marble tables that had once belonged to Caesar and beds that were owned by the Medici. He even had one of the reception halls, a space with outrageously high ceilings and a terrace facing the sea, excavated to house an indoor swimming pool. Sadly, Getty's tenure in what was often described as his most beloved house was cut short by the infamous kidnapping of his grandson, whose ear was cut off and mailed to his rich grandfather to convince him of the kidnapper's seriousness. Getty paid, left Italy in anger and swore never to return.

La Posta Vecchia was sold, at auction, to a family involved in hospitality and they set about turning it – complete with the entire inventory of antiquities – into a family beach house. Once their children had grown up, they decided to transform their beach house into a hotel, or rather a boutique hotel with grandeur – a 'baby grand'! The same family also owns Il Pellicano in Porto Ercole, one of the most famous hotels in Italy, and so was well equipped to know what to do.

I have visited on three occasions, twice by myself and once with my children, and it is always a delight. Part of the magic is the unlikely combination of beach and palazzo. You just don't expect to find a Renaissance 'anything' on the beach, and certainly not a palazzo with solid marble bathtubs and beds that Maria de' Medici slept in. Perhaps most importantly, the family understands that, once you get here, you are not going to want to leave, so the food and the service had better be up to scratch – as good as the architecture, the history and the setting. And it is.

UMBRIA

UMBRIA

UMBRIA IS KNOWN AS THE 'GREEN HEART' OF ITALY. FOOD IS MORE IMPORTANT HERE THAN ANYTHING ELSE – EXCEPT, PERHAPS, SPIRITUALITY.

PAX

Gubbio

Borgo di Carpiano

Perugia

Assisi

Norcia

Eremito

Spoleto

Orvieto

MONKS AS
WE KNOW THEM
ORIGINATED HERE:
NORCIA CREATED THE ORDER
OF SAINT BENEDICT, AND ASSISI
GAVE THE WORLD THE FRANCISCAN MONK.
FITTINGLY, THE MEDAL OF SAINT BENEDICT
PLOTS ALL THE UMBRIAN TOWNS WORTH VISITING.

The
Spiritual Heart
of Italy

Within a couple of hours' drive from Rome you can disappear into an Italy of rolling hills, mountains, forests, unpaved roads and medieval hamlets; an Italy barely touched by modernity, without high-rise buildings, *autostrade*, street lamps or supermarkets. Here, it is like going back in time to a world that frees the mind and soul. You probably think I'm talking about Tuscany, but I'm not. I am referring to Umbria. Twenty years ago, few people had heard of this landlocked part of Italy. Now Umbria is threatening to take over from Tuscany as the place to visit for food, for historic hilltop villages, and for rolling farmland topped with neat rows of cypress-pines.

To be honest, Umbria and Tuscany are very similar. They are direct neighbours, after all. Umbria does not have a city to match Florence, but in a way that's the point. Umbria is the green heart of Italy. As important as food and wine are to Tuscany, they seem even more important to Umbria. It's a subtle difference, but one that can definitely be felt in the experience of travelling around and eating – and, indeed, in how much it costs to travel around and eat! Umbria is significantly cheaper and fundamentally more accessible than Tuscany.

There is another factor at play here, and that is Umbria's spiritual heritage. This is the part of Italy that gave the world St Francis of Assisi, the monk who rejected the pomp and circumstance of the Catholic Church and became a champion of the poor; in the early 13th century he gave up all his worldly possessions and devoted his life to serving God, thus also laying the foundations of the Franciscan Order. It may not be overt, but the tone and message of St Francis of Assisi can be felt in Umbria. Everything is simpler, more down-to-earth, less grand. And that, I think, has struck a chord with a new generation of travellers.

EREMITO

Life without Distractions

A few years ago, I received a call from Marcello Murzilli, a wonderfully eccentric Italian whom I had first met in Mexico. 'Airrbert', he started, with his singing accent, 'it's me, Marcello – do you remember me?' 'Of course Marcello, how could I forget?' I replied in all honesty. How, indeed, could I forget the guy with the 'hanky' on his head, the man who had started the jeans brand El Charro and sold it for millions, sailed a boat halfway around the world and then come to a stop in Mexico. There, he couldn't resist buying a patch of jungle on a stretch of beach that had the most beautiful lagoon – completely inaccessible, but that didn't stop Marcello. He chopped through the jungle with machetes, built a road and created a compound of beautiful thatched stilt huts without any mod cons whatsoever – no electricity, no phones, no air conditioning. He called it Hotelito Desconocido (Little Undiscovered Hotel). It was a crazy gamble but it paid off, with rich bankers and hedge-fund managers queuing up to rediscover their inner boy scout. I spent quite some time with Marcello, and I will never forget meeting him at the top of his handmade watchtower, before dawn, to see the sun rise over the lagoon – his lagoon.

Several years had passed since we last spoke. He was back in Italy, having sold Hotelito Desconocido, and he wanted me to come and see his new place in Umbria, Eremito. 'It is something that has never been done before,' he said, and I believed him. Of course I did – it was Marcello! So I went to visit him at Eremito.

It came as no surprise that Eremito was extremely hard to find, and I'm sure that's just how Marcello likes it. I can honestly say that I have never spent so long on a dirt road anywhere in Italy. I had no idea that parts of Umbria could still be so remote. But finally, there it was, at the end of a very long and bumpy track: an austere stone building nestled in the folds of forest-clad hills. From a distance it looked like a forgotten monastery...very *Name of the Rose*.

You enter through a thick wooden gate suspended in a rough stone arch, which leads to a smaller but equally solid wooden door. Inside the dark, tunnel-like entrance, the first sound that greets you is Gregorian chanting, which I found a little spooky. It was late and Marcello had already gone to bed, so I decided to turn in as well. My room – or, more accurately, my cell – was a narrow rectangular space with an alcove just big enough for a slim single bed, a built-in desk by a solitary, slender window, and a marble washbasin suspended from the wall that looked more suited to baptisms than washing; there was also a small cubicle with a shower and toilet. If austerity was Marcello's new theme, I thought to myself, then he had succeeded admirably.

I awoke to a beautiful spring morning. Breakfast was served at a massive refectory table under a tree with a splendid view of the valley below. Together with the other guests I ate freshly baked bread and organic fruit surrounded by nothing but the pristine landscape of remote Umbria; there was not a single house or road or street lamp or electricity pole in sight. In between bouts of reminiscing, Marcello introduced me to two Franciscan monks, fellow guests. Part of the culture of Eremito is that monks stay for free. It was an unusual experience, but also fascinating. When was the last time you had breakfast with a monk?

Eremito means 'hermit' in Italian and seems entirely appropriate for a place that offers a taste of the hermit tradition, removed from civilization and the distractions of daily life. Guests stay in *celluzze* (monks' cells), with one guest per cell. There are no exceptions. If you arrive with a partner, you will each get your own cell. It's not possible to sleep together (in any case, it would run contrary to the whole 'experience'), although there certainly seemed to be a lot of doors opening and closing in the night...

Marcello built the place from scratch, from the remains of an abandoned farmhouse, with 130,000 stones laid according to a method of masonry dating from the 13th century. He did a brilliant job because it looks and feels like it has been here, in this isolated spot, forever. The only music to be heard (and allowed) in the handsomely austere spaces is Gregorian chanting. You won't get a mobile phone signal, and electronic devices are so frowned upon that they might as well be banned.

After breakfast you can go hiking in the surrounding hills or, weather permitting, swim in the nearby waterfall, which is exactly what I did. The waterfall is exquisite – tall, forceful, thunderous – and the water, which comes straight from the mountains, is so cold that even if you're not religious you will feel reborn. Lunch is served at the same location as breakfast, and the prevailing signature is 'no-nonsense hospitality'. You eat what is put on the table – all seasonal and fresh (and delicious) – and you drink what they pour from handmade terracotta jugs (water and red wine). It's strangely liberating not to have to make choices.

In the afternoon most guests choose to read on the grassy terrace (which you can read as: they fall asleep in the sun), but there is also a splendid spa. This is not a day spa in the modern sense, where you are pampered and spoilt rotten; it is a spa in the traditional sense of the word with a focus on wellness, a restorative space for body and mind. Here you can unwind in the steam bath or hot tub, and free yourself from the stresses of modern-day life.

So far so good. Life as a hermit was not bad, not bad at all. I had no decisions to make, and there was plenty of fresh air, seasonal food, beautiful views and interesting people to talk to. But then came dinner... Every night dinner is held in silence. And by that, I mean you are not allowed to say anything, and neither are the people who serve you. You sit on benches – in one long line – with no one facing you. It is hard to keep quiet when the piped Gregorian chanting starts to roll into cover versions of old Take That songs. Who knew there was such a thing? A guest to my left recognized the tune that the monks were chanting in Latin, and we were like schoolchildren desperately trying not to giggle. No one wants to be the one who can't keep his mouth shut! When dinner is finished and you have left the table, you can speak again. Most guests use the opportunity to meet for coffee on the grassy terrace, by which point they are generally talking as if their lives depended on it.

Marcello takes his new venture very seriously indeed, that much is clear, but he is definitely on to something. This kind of hermetic experience is a great adventure. A few days later, as I made my way back to civilization along that seemingly endless dirt road, I was smiling to myself. Marcello was right when he said that no one else has done anything like this, and to my surprise I can't remember when I had so much fun.

I love guys like Marcello. They make the world a more interesting place because they have the courage and the stamina to follow their convictions, no matter how unconventional they may seem.

BORGO DI CARPIANO

An Abandoned Hamlet Given a Second Life

From a distance, no one would guess that Borgo di Carpiano is a hotel with an award-winning restaurant. But that's exactly the appeal. It encapsulates a new approach to tourism – the idea of 'touching the earth lightly', of presenting an experience to the visitor that is as genuine as it can get, without sacrificing comfort or style. And by not disturbing the natural order of things, you – the visitor – connect more strongly with this authentic slice of Umbrian countryside.

Riccardo and Marilisa Parisi – the couple who transformed Carpiano from a dilapidated village into a unique place to stay – honed their hospitality skills in the Caribbean, on the island of Antigua. But they started to long for home, so they returned to Italy. Having spent months on the road looking for the right place, eventually they found this abandoned village in the countryside near the medieval town of Gubbio. Judging from the 'before' photos, the work required was epic, but none of that is visible now. Guests are presented with an immaculate antique stone village with lovely cottages, a wonderful restaurant and a beautiful pool tucked into the folds of the rolling hills.

The church, as always, is at the centre of the village, but masses are no longer held here. Carpiano's church, originally dedicated to St Blaise (San Biagio), was deconsecrated and now serves as a very grand living room and a suitably chic and unusual reception area – not something you would imagine from the outside. The same goes for the accommodation. The tiny cottages that once housed farm workers now have four-poster beds and stylish bathrooms. Many of the cottages also have their own gardens, but from a distance they still look like the stacked stone cottages that are so typical of Umbria's rustic hilltop villages.

Borgo di Carpiano is discreet in its approach and appearance, but not in its attitude to food. Eating and drinking are a big – if not the biggest – part of the equation. Umbria is known as the green heart of Italy, and food is taken very seriously in these parts. Borgo di Carpiano adheres to this tradition with an elaborate kitchen garden, their own olive trees and fruit orchards, and people in the kitchen who love to cook. In the summer, meals are served al fresco on a terrace that looks out over a landscape of rolling hills, and in the cooler months you eat by the fire in the restaurant, which used to be the hayloft. One thing that never changes, irrespective of the season, is the time and effort invested in the food at Borgo di Carpiano – a reason in itself for coming here.

SARDINIA

A Wild and
Isolated Place

In his book *Sea and Sardinia*, D. H. Lawrence described this island as a wild and isolated place, and even though he was writing in 1921 his words still ring true. Most of the population is concentrated in the cities of Olbia in the north, Cagliari in the south, and Alghero in the centre, on the west coast. The rest of the island is, for the most part, as empty and untouched as it was in Lawrence's day. Sardinia is a place of raw landscapes, with dense forests, craggy mountains, dark blue lakes, rolling sand dunes, rocky coasts, white beaches and turquoise seas.

It is not possible to write about Sardinia without looking at the island's unique heritage. Long before Phoenician merchants established the trading port of Cagliari (around 1000 BC), and the later armies from Carthage and Rome landed here, the island had an animist culture that was the most advanced of any in the Mediterranean. The Nuragic culture, which takes its name from the tower-shaped stone structures found on the island, thrived during the Bronze Age. The *nuraghi* towers, which are believed to have been used for worship, have roofs that open to the sky – prompting the theory that they were intended as observatories. Whatever their function, they were certainly built in large numbers. Today there are thousands dotted across the countryside in various states of ruin, and that's just the ones that we know of.

The conquering empires of the ancient Mediterranean seem to have had little effect on Sardinia, bar the odd well-preserved Roman temple to be found near cities such as Cagliari. Perhaps the rugged terrain proved too much of a challenge or the Sardinian people, who are famously stubborn, put up too much resistance. One thing is certain: Sardinians are a tough lot. That's because, until very recently, life was hard. The Nobel Prize-winning author Grazia Deledda, who was born in Nuoro in the mountains of central Sardinia in the late 1800s, writes about losing a younger sister to the harshness of a particularly cold winter.

This may explain why today, with heating and plumbing as a given, the inhabitants of the villages live so long. In recent years the island has had a lot of press that has nothing to do with tourism and everything to do with lifestyle. Locals typically reach their mid-nineties without skipping a beat.

L'AGNATA DI DE ANDRÉ

Former Home of Italy's Answer to Bob Dylan

Fabrizio De André was the Bob Dylan of Italy. When he was at the height of his fame, in the 1970s, he could have anything he wanted, but all he really wanted was to be a farmer. So he opted out of his 'rock star' life and bought a remote farm in the picturesque mountains of northern Sardinia, a few miles from Tempio Pausania. He dug his own lake, excavated an extraordinary rock pool for swimming, and grew ivy over everything. The farm, L'Agnata, was both his opus and his muse.

L'Agnata had a profound influence on De André's music. This is where he made the seminal album *Créuza de mä*, released in 1984, but it was also the scene of a truly shocking incident in De André's life. In August 1979, he and his girlfriend, the folksinger Dori Ghezzi, were kidnapped and taken to a spot in the nearby Alà dei Sardi mountains. Despite a massive manhunt aided by police from the mainland, they could not be found. After several months the family paid the substantial ransom, and Fabrizio De André and Dori Ghezzi were returned unharmed. If nothing else, the incident showed just how wild Sardinia still is. Despite the fact that De André and Ghezzi were being held less than an hour away from his farm, the police couldn't find them. Once the kidnappers had been caught, the liberally minded, socially conscious singer, in typical fashion, showed

solidarity with his kidnappers, declaring at their trial: 'They were the real prisoners, not I.'

Any other star, having experienced such an ordeal, might have become a security-obsessed recluse, but De André returned to his farm and on weekends he continued his custom of inviting locals from Tempio Pausania to eat with him at the house.

Sadly, De André died from cancer in 1999, at the relatively young age of fifty-eight. Twenty thousand people turned out for his funeral in Genoa, the town of his birth, and his widow (he married Ghezzi in 1989) decided to immortalize his legacy by opening L'Agnata as a restaurant and a retreat.

I had heard that the farm was once home to a rock star but knew none of the backstory when I first travelled to L'Agnata. It's not easy to find, and I was struggling. There are no signs here, no mobile phone reception, and the road leading to the farm is still unpaved. After my fifth wrong turn, I couldn't help wondering what would possess someone to buy in such an awkward location. But when I learned about Fabrizio De André, I admit, I started to see L'Agnata in a different light. I fell for the man and the place.

L'Agnata di De André is not the kind of place you go to if you like to be kept busy. You can go hiking or mountain biking or drive into town,

but most of the time you eat, you sleep, you swim...it's as simple as that. You might imagine that such remoteness is a disadvantage but the opposite is true. The effort involved in getting here somehow reaffirms how special it is. Despite its isolation, the restaurant – open only on weekends for non-guests – is very well known and the vibe, predictably, is laidback but sophisticated. The hotel, too, is popular, surviving, it seems, almost entirely on word of mouth. Fabrizio De André may be gone but his infectious free spirit lives on at L'Agnata. You won't find anything like this anywhere in Italy, or indeed anywhere else in the world.

FARO CAPO-SPARTIVENTO

The Seclusion of a Real Lighthouse

Getting to this extraordinary *faro*, or lighthouse, perched on a rocky promontory on the very tip of southern Sardinia, may seem relatively straightforward. You drive south, and keep going until the road ends. But then it does get a little more complicated because the unpaved road that leads to the lighthouse is barred. You have to have special government permission to go any further. Only officers of the Italian navy – the only ones authorized to adjust, reset or repair the beacon – and lucky guests are allowed through. As a result of the Italian government and maritime regulations regarding the security of lighthouses, Faro Capo-Spartivento is as exclusive and private as it gets, and must surely rank as one of the most unusual properties ever to be converted into a hotel.

Built in 1854, at the command of Victor Emmanuel II – whose initials are still emblazoned on the stone arch of the entrance – the lighthouse repeatedly came under fire from the Allies during the Second World War due to its strategic location. After the war it was restored and continued its important function of guiding ships at sea. The lighthouse was manned by a keeper until the 1980s but was then automated.

In 2006, Capo Faro-Spartivento attracted the attention of a local property developer and entrepreneur. The 'house' part of the lighthouse had deteriorated significantly, but eight years of fastidious work – under the watchful eye of the appropriately named architect Mario Dal Molin – has transformed the once sober and utilitarian building into an elegant and highly unusual hideaway. Outside it still looks the same, albeit in better condition, but inside it's a design dream. It helps, of course, that the proprietor and instigator of this peerless renovation – Alessio Raggio – is someone the *New York Times* described as 'the André Balazs of southern Sardinia'. He has been behind a number of enterprises in Cagliari, including Caffè de Candia, a bar in the newly revitalized part of the old walled city, Castello.

A lighthouse is limited in terms of available space, so it was never going to be a big hotel – a restriction that Raggio has used to his advantage by making it as upmarket as possible. That's why the infinity pool, sunk into a decked terrace that looks out to sea, seems to cantilever from the rocky cliffs; and why the roof – a 250 m^2 space surrounding the lantern, with extraordinary views in all directions – is fitted with elegant canopied daybeds intended for private sunbathing and watching the sun set; and why the six suites are white and modern and equipped with every convenience a demanding customer could want.

But what really sets this place apart is the location. Surrounded by sandy beaches, with

the best views in Sardinia, this lighthouse is for travellers who take hedonism seriously. Is it expensive? Hell, yeah! But for me there would be no choice between spending two nights here and going somewhere mediocre for a week.

Just one piece of advice: if you do plan to come here, don't come alone because you won't meet people or make friends. The guests at this *faro* are paying for the ultimate in privacy, and judging from my brief stay, they go out of their way to avoid contact with other guests. It's a romantic spot – one of the most romantic in Italy – and it's perfect for married couples... and I don't necessarily mean people married to each other. How very D. H. Lawrence! He would have loved it.

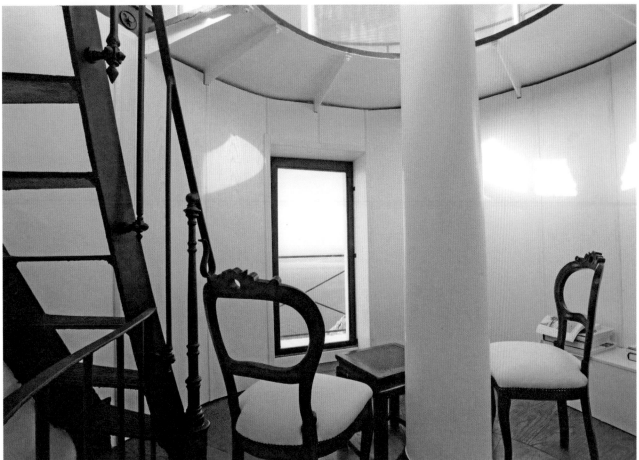

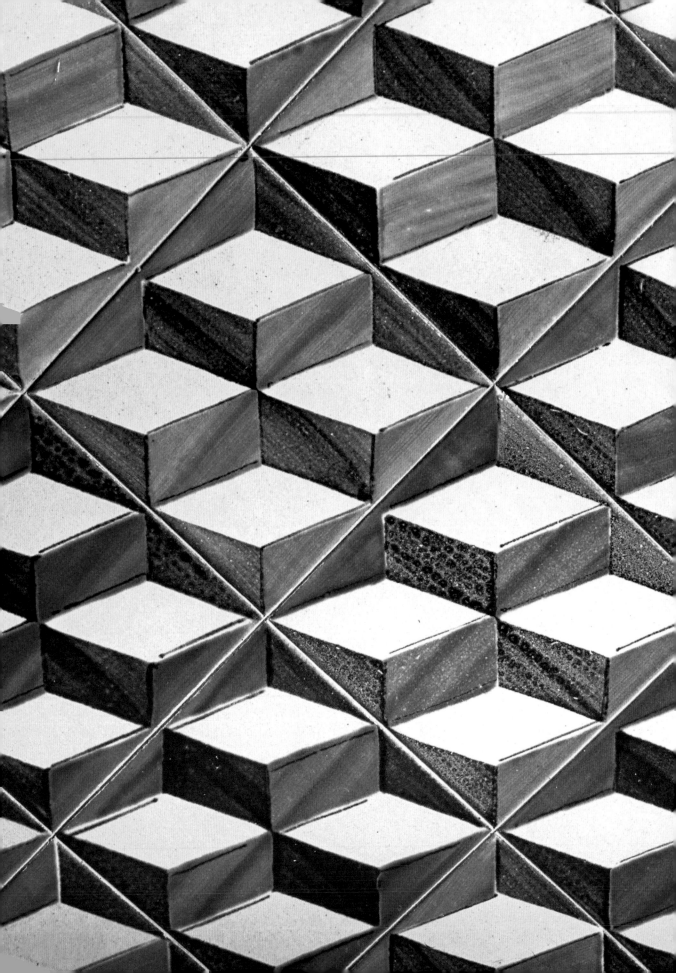

FLORENCE

AND

TUSCANY

FLORENCE

Visit the centre before 10 a.m.

Medici Palace

Cycle around the Duomo after 6 p.m.

ARNO

Head to the Oltrarno after lunch.

FLORENCE GAVE THE WORLD THE RENAISSANCE. A CITY THAT PULLED US OUT OF THE DARK AGES IS CLEARLY WORTH A VISIT, BUT TO ENJOY THE EXPERIENCE YOU HAVE TO RESORT TO STRATEGY AND STEALTH. A TIMEPIECE IS MORE USEFUL THAN A MAP, SO THAT YOU CAN TIME YOUR VISIT TO AVOID THE CROWDS.

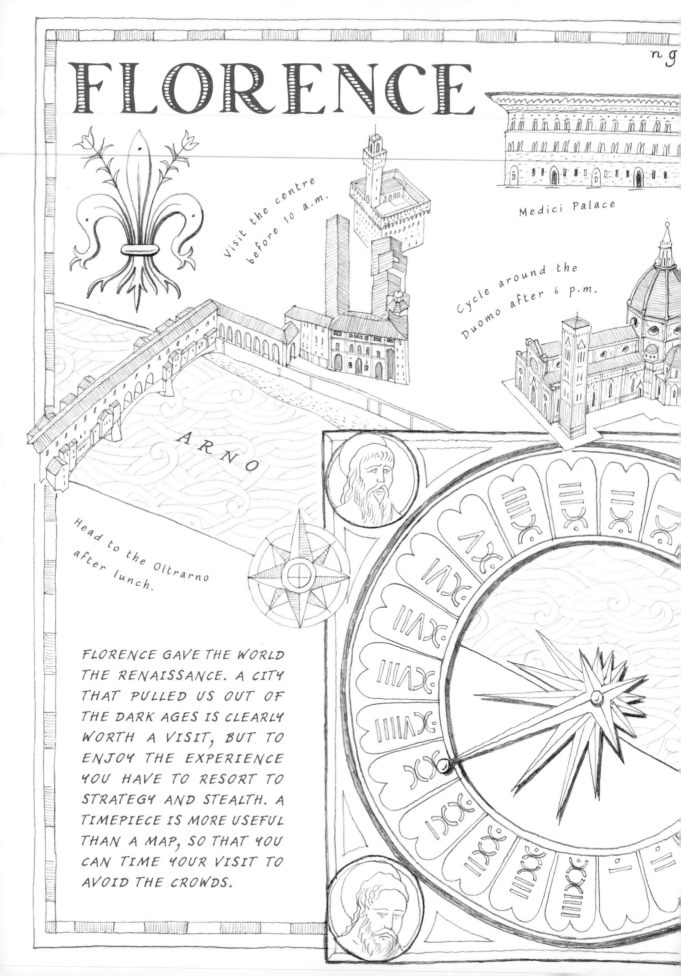

Florence:
The Athens of the
Middle Ages

Michelangelo, Leonardo da Vinci, Donatello, Fra Angelico, Botticelli, Benvenuto Cellini, Raphael, Benozzo Gozzoli, Peter Paul Rubens, Bronzino, Lorenzo Ghiberti... these are just some of the artists who worked in Florence during the Renaissance. It was a time when the city dominated the world's production of cloth and textiles, and minted Europe's strongest currency; when famous merchant families such as the Medici created new ways of conducting commerce and banking, and channelled their wealth into art. The cultural rebirth that began here was of such magnitude that even today, many centuries later, the city still has the greatest concentration of art in the world.

Not long ago I read an article in *The Australian* by a journalist recounting his first trip to Florence. He writes how he had been looking forward to his first 'face to face' with Renaissance art and architecture – seeing the works of Michelangelo, Da Vinci, Botticelli, Brunelleschi and the like in the flesh, instead of in books. All he wanted, he writes, was 'a room with a view' (romantic, but not particularly original) and the time to let it all sink in slowly and magnificently. It was a noble plan, but it proved a bit of a struggle. He found Florence to be 'cold and old and aloof'. He enjoyed the art, but not the experience.

He is not the first to have felt this way about Florence, and he won't be the last. Every year, this city that started the Renaissance, and boasts some of the most visited museums in Italy, gets swamped by an estimated 13 million visitors – roughly thirty-four times its own population. Given these statistics, it's understandable why locals don't always welcome tourists with open arms.

So what's the solution? How do you enjoy Florence without feeling like you're just another tourist? There's a great saying: 'If we all chose the same direction in life, the world would capsize.' What we need to do is choose a different direction, away from mainstream tourism. And it's easier than you might think...

THE SPARK THAT IGNITED THE RENAISSANCE

Dominating the city's skyline, the great dome of Santa Maria del Fiore was the spark that ignited the Renaissance. When the Wool Guild of Florence chose Neri di Fioravante's model of a dome, constructed without the aid of flying buttresses, in 1367, it marked the first 'event' of the Renaissance. It was a break with Gothic medieval architecture, but it was really much more than that. It marked the beginning of a new way of thinking – one that took inspiration from classical antiquity but challenged the beliefs and ideas of the past. The choice to go with this huge dome, the likes of which had never been attempted, necessitated a new approach.

The plans for the cathedral were ambitious, to say the least. The city demanded a place of worship that was larger and more spectacular than those of its rivals, Siena and Pisa, and so commissioned the mother of all cathedrals. It wasn't clear just how they would build it, but for the first time since the fall of the Roman Empire they started to look further afield for the answers. Several ancient ruins were studied, including the Pantheon in Rome, which features a large dome built using innovative concrete lozenges set within wooden frames. The Duomo ultimately proved too big to use the same approach, but at least Florence's architects were looking at sources that a few decades earlier might have been considered sacrilegious. The pattern was set. Innovation and imagination would be the key going forward.

The Duomo was the result of several design competitions and consumed a string of architects with fancy names. (A young Leonardo da Vinci also contributed to one aspect of the project: the copper ball that sits on the lantern at the top of the dome.) But its success rested on the genius of one man: Filippo Brunelleschi, the brilliant architect-engineer who worked out how Neri's dome could be achieved. He invented machines to hoist the 37,000 tons of materials – including four million bricks – used in its construction. It took 140 years to build the cathedral, which was finally consecrated in 1436, and a further 400 years to complete the façade. But once completed, the Duomo set every record imaginable for the time. It was the tallest cathedral in the world, with the widest dome, the highest internal ceiling and the longest nave.

So, when you visit Florence and look up at Brunelleschi's towering masterpiece, please don't think of this as yet another in a long line of extravagant European churches that almost broke the bank. Think of it, instead, as the laboratory that got us out of the Dark Ages.

OUTSIDE FIRST

The Best Place to Start

The first thing most visitors to Florence do is scramble for tickets to the Uffizi Gallery. I've never understood that, because the most impressive things to see and experience in this city are outside – starting, of course, with the Duomo, along with the many other significant buildings and sculptures dotted around town. One example is Michelangelo's *David*, outside the Palazzo Vecchio, a former residence of the Medici family that now serves as the town hall. Okay, the statue is a copy, but does that matter? It's a faithful copy in every sense. Only an art expert might be able to tell the difference. You can't help but admire the scale and the subtlety and the restraint of the artist in sculpting a statue intended to depict a weaker man, courageous enough to take on a bigger, stronger one, but that's why it's so famous.

Then there are the sculptures that line the Loggia dei Lanzi, an open-air building that lies adjacent to Palazzo Vecchio – originally called Palazzo della Signoria after the governing body that ruled Florence during the medieval and Renaissance periods. The works by artists such as Benvenuto Cellini and Giambologna are carved from massive blocks of Carrara marble and depict mythical scenes. Unlike a museum, you can get as close as you want (without touching, obviously) and take as many pictures as you see fit. Most importantly, when you've had enough, it won't be more than five minutes before you are sitting on the terrace of a café, discussing the progress of your outdoor cultural safari. You are under no obligation to see it all – far better to grasp a few masterpieces than to rush through so many that they become a blur.

IL BORRO TUSCAN BISTRO

Ham, cheese, sausages, potatoes, beef and olive oil are the ingredients of Tuscan food.

IF YOU ARE EATING SPAGHETTI, PIZZA, OR MOZZARELLA AND TOMATO IN FLORENCE, YOU ARE NOT EATING TUSCAN FOOD. THE CUISINE OF 'TOSCANA' IS HEARTY AND BASIC, ORIGINATING

This bistro takes its name from an Italian village.

IN THE VILLAGES. AND THE BEST VILLAGE IS THE ONE OWNED BY THE FERRAGAMO FAMILY – THE VILLAGE THAT SUPPLIES THEIR TUSCAN BISTRO IN FLORENCE.

THE SAVOY

The 'Groovy Grand' Alternative

The Savoy is quite simply the best hotel in Florence – minutes from the Duomo, Palazzo Vecchio and Michelangelo's *David*, and on the same street as the most elegant shops. It combines the beauty and history of Florence with a casual, informal elegance that is very much the hallmark of the modern-day city. Although grand in terms of location, architecture and service, it is not stuffy or pretentious in the slightest. It's not trying to give you 'Medici revisited' – to recreate the artistic splendour of the Renaissance – inside its own walls. Why should it? You are in Florence, the city that started the Renaissance. You can visit the real thing just around the corner. Instead, what has been most carefully conceived and calibrated is the 'experience'.

In the morning, instead of a grand dining room with chandeliers, breakfast is served in a funky, modern bistro-bar called 'Irene' with a terrace that opens directly onto Piazza della Repubblica – something much more in step with the city's long-standing connection to fashion. Irene looks and feels like somewhere the modish crowd would frequent – and they do. I also like the fact that the guest rooms are bright and colourful and modern in a sophisticated, intelligent way, and yet you still get the marble bathroom that you were secretly hoping would be part of your Italian hotel experience. One thing the Savoy will not give you, and this is important: it will not give you the feeling that you're a tourist.

SIP AN *APERITIVO* ON A ROOFTOP

In medieval times, important families used their immense wealth not only to build extravagant palazzi, but also towers – which were often attached to their inner-city palaces. These were brick monoliths with few windows and extraordinarily thick walls, and secret entrances and passageways just in case a family should find itself under siege. It was a place of safety – somewhere they could retreat to if they were in danger.

One surviving example, the Consorti tower, now forms part of the Hotel Continentale and houses a roof terrace – La Terrazza – with one of the best views in Florence. La Terrazza looks out over the River Arno and the Ponte Vecchio, immediately below, and the famous watchtower of Palazzo Vecchio – the one featured in just about every film or drama centring on the eventful lives of the Medici family – is squarely in front of you, with the omnipresent dome of Santa Maria del Fiore in the distance. All the architectural masterpieces for which Florence is famed are here, in one sweeping panorama. You would never know that the terrace existed, certainly not from the street, but it's the best place for an *aperitivo*. The fact that it also has some genuine historical precedence makes it that much more authentic and meaningful as an experience.

You can also stay at the top of the Consorti tower. The Consorti suite is a duplex, with a canopy bed and living area downstairs and a bathroom upstairs. One of the bathroom windows frames the Duomo beautifully. I can't imagine a more historic, more stylishly luxurious and more private vantage point anywhere in the city. Hundreds of years ago, a Florentine family would have used this tower to hide from its enemies; today, you can use it to hide from all the tourists.

RIVA LOFTS

An Architect's Eye Applied to Former Leather Workshops

On the banks of the River Arno, in the Oltrarno district (meaning the 'other' side of the Arno), these former artisan workshops were initially converted by Florentine architect Claudio Nardi, in 1999, to function as his home and his studio. Eventually, his practice and his family outgrew the space, and he decided to move elsewhere. The quasi-industrial spaces were then converted, beautifully, into an exquisite collection of lofts for visitors – for people who refuse to stay in a box, even for one night.

Given the amount of space, and the fact that there's a swimming pool in the garden and a wood-burning fireplace in the breakfast room, you might imagine Riva to be some distance from town, but it only took me fifteen minutes to get to my favourite stationer's near Palazzo Pitti, on one of the vintage bicycles that are made available at Riva. Riva is much more than a slick series of design spaces: it's an opportunity to feel like an artist in residence or a local with a cool pad.

CYCLE ALONG THE RIVER ARNO

Is it possible to visit Italy without setting foot in Florence? Perhaps. But you might always wonder what you missed out on. Thirteen million visitors per year surely can't be wrong, can they? But this is where the challenge lies. How can you possibly enjoy Florence without getting caught in a tourist trap? The answer is...a bicycle. Your own bicycle. Many people aren't aware that

Florence has been investing in alternative travel, which includes building a substantial cycle route along the River Arno. This is far more than a few dotted lines painted on a busy road; it is a proper, separate road for cyclists that runs along the length of the River Arno's path through Florence. Apart from the stunning and quite unique vista it provides as you glide along the

river towards the Ponte Vecchio and the ancient centre of Florence, it also takes you away from the congestion of inner-city Florence. There are now so many people milling about in this historic town that, at certain times of the day, it feels like Disneyland. That's not the memory you want from Florence.

If you want to experience Florence at its best, head in early while most tourists are still having breakfast and get out of town by 10 a.m. at the latest. Alternatively, opt for a lazy start and cycle in just before lunch. The cycle path goes straight past Il Borro, which solves the problem of where to have lunch. There is no better or more authentic place in Florence for Tuscan food. After lunch, cross the bridge in front of Il Borro and head to the part of Florence known as the Oltrarno, which is the decidedly less touristy and more authentic part of town. It has plenty of hidden piazzas, and cafés and shops – including Giulio Giannini & Figlio, established in 1856, which makes the most exquisite stationery, diaries and notebooks.

As the sun starts to go down, make your way back across the Arno, park your bike in the small courtyard in front of the Hotel Art and head towards the lifts of the all-white Hotel Continentale. Go to the top floor and you will emerge into the best roof bar in Florence. It's more than a bar – it's a viewing platform with alcohol, directly above the Ponte Vecchio.

Then, when most visitors start to return to their hotels or head out to dinner, it's time to get back on your bike and cycle around the Duomo – by far the best way to grasp the scale of this Renaissance masterpiece.

SOPRARNO SUITES

Eccentric Collector Reinvents 16th-century Townhouse

Once upon a time there was an eccentric Florentine lawyer named Matteo Perduca who couldn't stop collecting – 1950s furniture, Danish modern, industrial chic, road signs, toys and more. When his collections became unmanageably large, he opened a shop in the courtyard of a 16th-century townhouse in the funky Oltrarno district. The shop didn't work out, but when a few apartments became available on the first and second floors of this inner-city gem, he and his wife Betty Soldi, a British-born graphic designer, decided to use his collections to furnish and create what must be the most original B&B in Florence. Wit, eccentricity and quirky modernity have come to a historic palazzo a stone's throw from the Ponte Vecchio, the oldest and most famous footbridge in Florence.

There are grand rooms, with impossibly high ceilings, freestanding baths and oak floors.

There's a suite entirely decorated with toys, ranging from Lego figurines to vintage video consoles to old board games. There are lamps made from fire extinguishers, tables cut from zinc storage tanks and church pews turned into bookcases. There's a suite dedicated to maps, and a smaller one featuring French *toile de Jouy*. Needless to say, every room is different. You'll be surprised by the humour and amazed by the original architecture of this Renaissance gem. The staircase alone is worthy of a postcard back home. The one thing you won't be at this address is bored. It's a fascinating place that seems to attract 'interested' and 'interesting' people, and the breakfast, which is served in a quirky communal space with shared tables and odd signs, provides a wonderfully upbeat start to the day. (Do I need to mention the coffee? Well, of course it's great – this is Italy, after all.)

Tuscany: The Food, the History, the Wine ...and the Views

Every once in a while, the travel world announces a previously unheralded part of Italy as the 'new Tuscany', as if there's something wrong with the old Tuscany. It all seems somewhat pointless to me because there is only one Tuscany: a beautiful, ancient and surprisingly mountainous area of Italy that, despite some claims to the contrary, has not been spoiled.

Tuscany's enduring appeal lies in its natural beauty, its history, and its food and wine. It conjures up images of Medici opulence, of the ornate palazzi and cathedrals of great cities such as Florence, and of villas and carefully planted cypress-pines amid rolling hills. It is a landscape of peaks and valleys that divide one remote village from the next, but it is also a lot wilder than you might imagine. Tuscany is, I think, a little misunderstood. The Medici model isn't inaccurate – just narrow. So what is the 'real Tuscany'? This is not an easy question to answer. I have rented houses here, stayed on farms and in villages, and in famous hotels, but only now am I beginning to get some idea of what Tuscany is truly about.

Long before this region was made famous by the exploits of wealthy Renaissance families, when Rome was still plotting its rise to empire, it was settled by the Etruscans – a proud, strongly agricultural people famed for their skills as artisans and warriors. Etruscans were self-reliant and they established a tradition of independence and spirituality closely linked to the land. In a way, the Etruscans are to Tuscany what the Vikings were to Scandinavia: the core and the origin of a distinct cultural signature. The Etruscans set the pattern for what Tuscany would become: a tough, independently minded community of remote, isolated villages linked by common values that are underlined by a deep respect for, and understanding of, the land.

To experience the real Tuscany, you need to immerse yourself in its history and feel a connection to the land and its produce; you need to feel remote and isolated, just as the Etruscans would have felt. There are many charming and historic places to stay in this region, ranging from converted farmhouses to restored palazzi, but there are only two that I know of that deliver on every point.

BORGO SANTO PIETRO

A Village Rescued with Taste and Style

Once upon a time, a Danish couple – a property developer and a designer – went looking for a house in Tuscany and ended up buying an entire village. He, Claus Thottrup, then gave it to Jeanette Thottrup as a wedding present, and the die was cast for one of the most romantic places in Italy. The beauty that greets you now belies the work and the heartache that came before. In the first year, admits Jeanette, 'I woke up every morning in a sweat, wondering what we had got ourselves into.' Fixing up a house is one thing; tackling an entire village, quite another.

What the Thottrups have done with this village, which once housed five farming families, is nothing short of a revelation. I have seldom come across a project that is so in touch with its location and history or so connected to local traditions in food and medicine. The Thottrups can go back much further than the property's farming past: they know what was here hundreds of years ago (a quarantine house for pilgrims travelling to the shrine of Galgano) and even thousands of years ago (nearby tombstones reveal a strong Etruscan presence).

Set in 80-hectare grounds, this extraordinary hotel is a study in attention to detail and a poster child for the complete refusal to compromise. The food is acclaimed, the design is convincingly chic and the mood is romantic in a natural, authentic manner – exactly how you would want your own house in Tuscany to be. The bathrooms have features such as antique chandeliers, vintage velvet curtains and hand-carved marble basins. And the gardens, with their antique statuary and elegant fountains, could fill an entire book.

But the most outstanding quality of this restored, reconstructed and reconfigured village is the relationship with the land. Everything – and I mean everything – at Borgo Santo Pietro is connected to the surroundings. The pool, for instance, is nothing like a pool, but more like a little lake – with a strategically placed boulder here and an organic curve there – nestled into the folds of the land. You gaze out over rolling hills of farmland as you swim.

The experience on offer is total immersion in Tuscany, from the all-encompassing views to the handmade plates and homemade cheeses. The hotel organizes a range of activities, including guided walks, and even has a residency programme for established artists, who then provide classes in watercolour and landscape painting. If Borgo Santo Pietro were any more involved with Tuscany, it would be accredited as a cultural university. I don't think there's a better way to experience the real Tuscany, although it is not without risks to your waistline.

Wild dandelion
as a filling for
homemade ravioli

Wild chicory
for salads

CHEF ANDREA MATTEI IS A TUSCAN, AND THE
THINGS HE DOES – SUCH AS PLUCKING WILD
INGREDIENTS – HE DOES BECAUSE THAT'S
WHAT HE HAS ALWAYS DONE. TUSCANS ARE

From the passion for seasonal ingredients to the love of simple things, such as the bread on the table, not a detail is overlooked, not a nuance neglected.

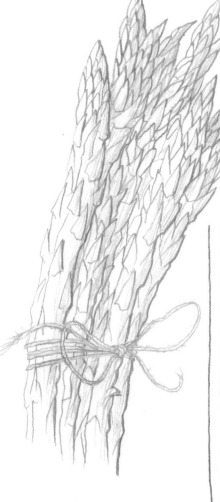

Wild asparagus for a frittata

CONNECTED TO THE LAND IN THE WAY THAT FISHERMEN ARE CONNECTED TO THE SEA. THEY APPRECIATE NATURE'S BOUNTY BECAUSE THEY HAVE GROWN UP WITH IT.

CASTELLO DI VICARELLO

12th-century Hilltop Castle with Oriental Treasures

When Aurora Baccheschi Berti was a little girl, she played in the ruins of a 12th-century castle, high on a hill in the remote Maremma region of Tuscany. Maremma means 'swamp' or 'marsh', and ever since the fall of Rome this part of Tuscany has seen the greatest drop in population. The wetlands were a breeding ground for malaria and other water-borne diseases, so, slowly, the population settled further inland and higher into the surrounding peaks. Over the centuries attempts were made to drain the swamps, most notably by the Medici during the Renaissance, but with little success. Today, these aborted plans have proved to be a blessing in disguise, with many visitors attracted to the region by its abundant wildlife, which includes pink flamingos.

As a young adult Aurora moved to Bali and set up a fashion business there. But after twenty years on this magical Hindu island, with her sons needing a more formal education, she returned to Italy with her family, and in an act of self-proclaimed insanity she and her husband Carlo decided to take on the monumental task of restoring the ruins of a 12th-century keep near the town of Montalcino – the very castle ruins she played in as a child. With the heirlooms from Carlo's family estate in Florence and numerous treasures brought back from Bali, the couple turned a pile of medieval stones on top of a hill into an exquisite home. It was never intended as anything other than a family house, but practicality dictated that they would have to rent out at least part of it to make the project sustainable. Part of the estate was thus earmarked as accommodation for paying guests.

Aside from its imposing location and extraordinary history, the property is distinguished by the owners' exquisite taste: a fantastically original, eccentric mix of ethnic pieces from Bali and hereditary antiques from Carlo's noble Florentine family. That's how a 12th-century castle in Tuscany with an oriental flair came to be one of the most original boutique hotels in Italy. Most importantly, it's as Tuscan as it gets.

Poised on top of a hill, Castello di Vicarello has sweeping panoramas in every direction, but none is better than the view from the infinity pool in the garden. I have seen beautiful pools before, but this is truly a gem – made all the more special because it is constructed entirely of travertine. It's not an obvious choice as this particular type of stone is quite porous, but it gives the water a milky light green colour, which is utterly in keeping with a pool that seems to touch the horizon.

MILAN

AND

LAKE COMO

Milan – Capital of Fashion

Milan is considered the city of style, the city of fashion. You might expect it to be like an Armani ad – full of beautiful, impeccably turned-out people saying 'ciao!' to each other all day long. But it's not. Milan is a working city, with pollution and traffic and construction and noise, and like most cities it has its fair share of unattractive office blocks, architectural blunders and eyesores. I have been to this city more times than I can remember – on my own, with my parents, for work, with my wife – and I know how tough it is for Milan to live up to everyone's expectations. Milan is not the Italian catwalk brought to life, but that doesn't mean it can't be.

Do Milan 'properly' and it can be just as you dreamt, perhaps even better. But be warned: this is not possible on a budget. If you're on a budget, take it out of your travel plans. 'Properly' means staying at the Bulgari Hotel and having dinner (at least once) in the hotel's celebrated restaurant, seeing a performance at La Scala, having lunch at Il Salumaio di Montenapoleone, and shopping at Italy's flagship boutiques on Via della Spiga and, to a lesser extent, Via Montenapoleone. There are other hotels and restaurants, of course, but I'm talking about making Milan more than memorable – making it perfect! Do this – even if you stay only for one night – and Milan will live up to all your fantasies.

BULGARI HOTEL

The Glamour of the Milan We All Dream About

The Bulgari is *the* hotel in Milan. There are other luxury hotels such as the Four Seasons, which occupies a very handsome former monastery on the aptly named Via Gesù, and of course there's the Grand Hotel et de Milan on Via Alessandro Manzoni, which is where Giuseppe Verdi lived (famous faces such as Luchino Visconti have also stayed here). These hotels are suitably grand, but I don't think you come to Milan for grand. You come here for glamour, and the most glamorous place – the only one that resembles a page from Italian *Vogue* – is the Bulgari Hotel.

If you hanker after the Milan of beautiful people, then the Bulgari is your only option. This is where they all hang out – the models, the tycoons, the intellectuals, the fading aristocracy. Why? Because it has one of the few gardens in the centre of Milan and is a place where you can eat and drink and mix with everyone who is anyone. In fact, if you are not staying at the hotel, I doubt you will get a table for dinner in the garden – it's as brutal as that.

With its Antonio Citterio-designed furniture, its Asian-inspired spa and its wonderful collection of vintage black-and-white Italian fashion photography from the 1950s and '60s, the Bulgari Hotel has created a world of its own in the heart of the city, and that is what you are paying for – plus the fact that this jewelry brand knows a thing or two about luxury. The experience will leave you with a decidedly warped and completely unrealistic impression of Milan, but who cares? You are here to indulge your fashion fantasies – reality can wait.

DUOMO DI MILANO

The Cathedral that Took 600 Years to Complete

Like its counterpart in Florence, the cathedral in Milan is known as the Duomo. It is one of the largest churches in the world and the largest church in Italy, excluding the Vatican. Remarkably, it took six centuries to complete, with the last bits of work finished as recently as 1965. For all its grandeur and Gothic excess, however, this dominant landmark has never been to everyone's taste. Many prominent critics, including John Ruskin, didn't have a kind word to say about it, but perhaps the most astute comment comes from Henry James, who wrote in his *Italian Hours* of 1909: 'A structure not supremely interesting, not logical, not...commandingly beautiful, but grandly curious and superbly rich... If it had no other distinction it would still have that of impressive, immeasurable achievement...a supreme embodiment of vigorous effort.'

James provides an interesting perspective from which to observe this monumental church. Despite an obsession with detail that informs every square inch of the building, the city of Milan still managed to finish it. To sustain a vision and a sense of purpose over six centuries seems particularly appropriate in a city so dedicated to work.

Facing the Piazza del Duomo is the Galleria Vittorio Emanuele II, a covered arcade with a soaring glass roof and magnificent floors of polished terrazzo. In the morning, when this Belle Epoque masterpiece is bathed in light, there is no better spot for a morning cappuccino. It's one of my favourite places to sit and watch Milanese life go by. Many of the shops are predictable – the usual global luxury brands – but it doesn't matter. It's the building itself that makes the experience special.

Duomo

IN THE MORNING, LIGHT STREAMS INTO THIS
COVERED ARCADE WITH ITS SOARING GLASS
ROOF AND MAGNIFICENT FLOORS OF POLISHED
TERRAZZO. THERE IS NO BETTER PLACE IN MILAN
TO SIT IN A CAFÉ AND WATCH THE WORLD GO BY.

La Scala

NOT ONLY IS THIS BELLE EPOQUE MASTERPIECE
ITALY'S OLDEST SURVIVING ARCADE – THE MOTHER
OF THE MODERN-DAY SHOPPING CENTRE – BUT
IT IS ALSO THE PASSAGEWAY THAT CONNECTS
LA SCALA TO THE DUOMO.

IL SALUMAIO DI MONTENAPOLEONE

Understated Sophistication in a Historic Courtyard

Let's assume you took my advice about doing Milan properly and you are spending one night at the Bulgari and two days in town. That means two lunches, one dinner, a few morning cappuccinos, and afternoon tea. One of your lunches has to be at Il Salumaio di Montenapoleone, a famous deli that has morphed into one of the city's most consistent and sophisticated restaurants. The name would suggest that it's located on Via Montenapoleone, but it isn't; it used to be, when it was still a deli. Now, it's on the quiet Via Santo Spirito, which connects Via Montenapoleone with Via della Spiga. From the outside it looks like it could be a consulate or perhaps a museum (which the rest of the building is). The front gate on Via Santo Spirito leads through a porte cochère to a surprisingly large cobbled courtyard. When the weather is fine, the ornate neoclassical courtyard is set with elegant wrought-iron tables and chairs and white linen tablecloths. A small army of immaculately clad waiters completes the picture.

The food is good, but I have read complaints from travellers that the menu is not particularly innovative. It is not supposed to be. You're in Milan. Italians are very happy with their cuisine. They don't want the distraction of chefs experimenting like mad scientists in the kitchen. Dried ice, smoke, and bizarre flavours and concoctions are not part of the Italian eating experience. If you can deliver a genuine *risotto alla Milanese* – complete with a tiny sliver of gold leaf on the top – like Mamma used to make at home, that's the sign of a good restaurant.

Como – It's all about the Lake!

When you write the story of two happy lovers,
let the story be set on the banks of Lake Como.

Franz Liszt

Lake Como has long attracted the cream of world tourism. It was a favourite escape for Napoleon, Queen Victoria, Tsar Nicholas II and just about every distinguished aristocrat on the Grand Tour, all drawn to its rare blend of majestic natural beauty and neoclassical splendour. William Wordsworth described Como as 'a treasure whom the earth / Keeps to herself', while Percy Bysshe Shelley, in 1818, wrote, 'This lake exceeds anything I ever beheld in beauty'. Mark Twain, who visited the lake in 1867, also provides a colourful description in his collection of travel stories, *The Innocents Abroad*. And in the first months of peace following the Second World War, Winston Churchill – of all the places he could have chosen – chose to come here, to relax and paint on the shores of the lake.

So what is it that has made Lake Como such an enduring magnet for travellers past and present? With Como, it is all about the lake. There is something magical about it – it mesmerizes and captivates. You can't tire of it because you never experience the same lake twice. Its beauty is constant, yet fluid. It changes in colour and in texture; with the skies, with the seasons and with the hours of the day. In winter, the lake is a symphony of solemn tones of grey. In spring, wild flowers provide bursts of colour in the surrounding mountain meadows, while the craggy peaks remain dusted with snow. In summer, the bright light and clear skies make the lake as blue as can be, and the water sparkles so intensely that it becomes a blinding sheet of pure silver.

Lake Como's natural beauty is captivating, but there is also something else at play here that is often overlooked: the role of man. Man has contributed to the enchantment of the lake, enhanced it even. The baroque palazzi with their elegant gardens, the charming churches and picturesque villages, and the colourful houses – painted red, yellow and ochre – all add to the alpine majesty to make this one of the most special places on the planet. Modest locals will tell you that there are some manmade structures around the lake that are not so pretty, but in a way this is the point: in the rest of the world people will comment on a building that is handsome or beautiful – on Lake Como they will talk about the few places that are not.

GRAND HOTEL TREMEZZO

The Best View of the Lake

Over the years, Lake Como has assembled its fair share of grand hotels. Villa d'Este, Tremezzo, Villa Serbelloni: all have a history of illustrious guests, and have swimming pools that seem to float in the lake or in the garden, or both, as well as elegantly manicured gardens and indulgent spa facilities. In the opulent chandelier-lit restaurants of these hotels, immaculate waiters clad in white dinner jackets provide the kind of impeccable service that only the Italians seem to be able to sustain. More recently, a couple of luxuriously contemporary, design-led hotels have also entered the fray, providing more choice.

However, if it's your first time at Lake Como, there is one hotel that beats the others hands down in terms of location and views: Grand Hotel Tremezzo. Located on the western shore, this hotel is on a stretch of the lake that boasts some of the most splendid palazzi and gardens, including the adjacent Villa Carlotta, set against a backdrop of soaring mountains. The view from the hotel takes in Bellagio straight ahead and, to the left, the widest point of the lake and the eastern shore beyond. No one would dispute that Bellagio is the most picturesque village on the lake, and it does have a few grand hotels of its own, including the sumptuous Villa Serbelloni, but the view *from* Bellagio is nowhere near as captivating as the view *of* Bellagio.

I have stayed at many hotels on Lake Como, but none has delivered the spectacle that Grand Hotel Tremezzo does. It is like a dedicated viewing platform – as if it were built solely for the view, which is not far from the truth. This was the first purpose-built hotel on the lake. It is not a palazzo converted into a hotel, but was inspired by the visit of a prominent Como family to the Universal Exposition of 1889, in Paris – the one for which the Eiffel Tower was built. Captivated by the idea of modernity, the family returned to Lake Como and decided to build a hotel in the Art Nouveau style. Modernity was at the heart of the project and became a motto of sorts for the charismatic matriarch of the family. When the Grand Hotel Tremezzo opened on 10 July 1910, it had all the mod cons, including electricity, central heating and a lift, but the most modern feature of all – the one that fascinated all who came to visit – was the fact that every room had its own bathroom.

The photos from the early 1900s, after the hotel first opened, are wonderfully revealing. Ladies in white linen and big hats on the tennis courts, out on the lake or taking tea on the terrace are testament not only to the success of the emancipated vision of the founding family, but also to how little has changed in terms of the gardens, the building and the view.

BELLAGIO

The Most Famous Little Town in Italy

From the western shore, the quaint town of Bellagio looks positively miniature, dwarfed by the Grigne mountains in the distance: a tiny, hazy cluster of buildings and church towers packed onto a peninsula that juts out into the lake. And by water is exactly how you should approach this picture-perfect village. In the calm of dawn, ferries and boats heading to and from Bellagio leave a spiderweb of tracks, momentarily turning the lake into a giant Etch a Sketch. As you get closer, a wonderful sense of anticipation builds as fuzzy features turn into houses, churches, streets, gardens and pavilions, with the omnipresent mountains looming ever taller. I really can't imagine getting here any other way than by water. In fact, if you choose to arrive by car

– driving along the southern shore from the town of Como – you won't see anything of Bellagio because by the time you get close enough, the road is closed to traffic. You have to park and walk the rest of the way, and you will have missed the theatre of the slow reveal.

You certainly don't need to have your own boat to experience Bellagio fully. The effect is the same whether you travel by Riva boat or by ferry. However, it is an experience that will be forever etched into your mind. Bellagio is more idyllic, more charming and more splendidly situated than anything I could have imagined. No wonder Bellagio was the name chosen for the most spectacular casino in Las Vegas. It has become a byword for impressive classic beauty.

VERONA

AND

LAKE GARDA

Crossroads
of the
Ancient World

Verona was one of the most important towns of the Roman Empire. It lay at the intersection of three significant Roman roads – the Postumia, the Gallica and the Claudia Augusta – and was considered a crossroads between the various peoples and cultures of the ancient world: the Goths to the north, the Gauls to the west, Byzantium to the east, and Rome, of course, to the south.

What's remarkable about this northern outpost is how well its Roman heritage has been preserved. Perhaps even the invading barbarians recognized its crucial role as a crossroads and spared it. The Roman Arena is almost completely intact, and there is even a Roman road – running a few metres below a street in the city centre – so perfectly preserved that you can see the grooves worn into the stone from centuries of iron-banded wooden wagon wheels rolling along its surface. Of all the historic cities in Italy, Verona may not be the largest or the most important, but it is certainly one of the prettiest.

SEE AN OPERA IN A ROMAN ARENA

Verona's Arena is the third largest Roman amphitheatre in the world and seated 30,000 spectators in its day. Only the arena in Capua and, of course, the Colosseum in Rome are bigger. Unlike the Colosseum, the Arena's interiors are remarkably intact – so well preserved, in fact, that it still hosts events, including the city's spectacular opera festival every summer. People come from far and wide to watch the lavish productions in a magical venue that is open to the sky.

During the day, Piazza Brà – which is home to the Arena, and Verona's largest public square – is used to store the monumental sets for the nightly productions. That is how, a few summers ago, I was able to photograph the Arena surrounded by the props for *Aida*; elaborate sphinxes, heroically sculpted lions, Egyptian chariots and towering pharaonic statues crowded the piazza, as if Antony and Cleopatra had arrived in Verona. Best of all, none of it was protected or guarded or hidden from view. People cycled by, children played on the pieces, climbed on them, ran their hands along them, and nobody raised an eyebrow. Where else in the world would you find such ease with culture? Erica Jong was right when she said that Italy, unlike most countries, still allows people to be human.

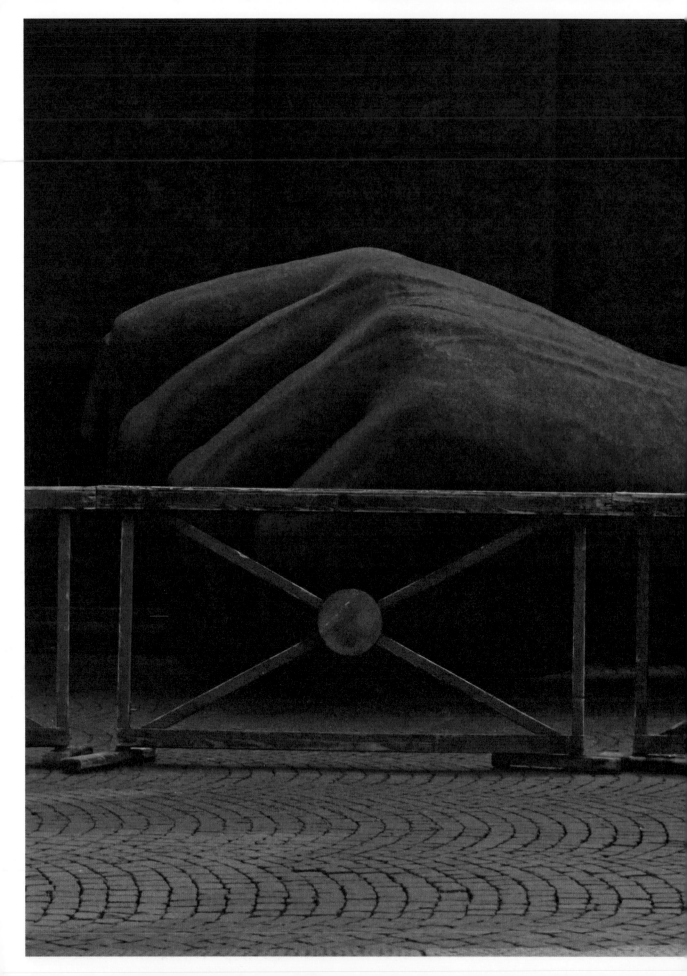

In the late 1950s Carlo Scarpa set about restoring the medieval Castelvecchio Museum in Verona, which had been damaged during the war. With its delicate balance between the old and the new, it is one of the Venetian architect's most poetic works.

SHAKESPEARE SET THREE OF HIS PLAYS IN VERONA: ROMEO AND JULIET, THE TAMING OF THE SHREW AND THE TWO GENTLEMEN OF VERONA. THIS INNER-CITY BOUTIQUE

Roman Arena

HOTEL, INSPIRED BY SHAKESPEARE'S STORY-
TELLING, SITS IN THE HEART OF HISTORIC
VERONA, A STONE'S THROW FROM THE ARENA
AND CASTELVECCHIO.

VILLA FELTRINELLI

Doge for a Day

Not far from Verona, in the village of Gargnano, on the western shore of Lake Garda, stands the fabulously extravagant Villa Feltrinelli. Commissioned by the Feltrinelli family in 1892, the extensive waterfront estate includes a boathouse and Venetian-style docks, and fragrant *limonaie* (lemon groves) line the steep slopes behind the house. The Feltrinellis made their money in timber in the 19th century, but moved into paper manufacturing in the early 20th century and then into publishing, eventually establishing a chain of bookshops that can still be found all over Italy. In 1972, the Feltrinelli story took a dramatic and sinister turn when the heir to the family fortune, Giangiacomo Feltrinelli – a political anarchist – was blown up, having seemingly triggered his own explosives by mistake. The house was shuttered and the fabulous estate – by this time in disrepair – was put up for sale.

The property remained on the market for some years. Then along came Bob Burns, founder of the Regent hotel chain, who had just sold his company to the Four Seasons group. He bought Villa Feltrinelli with the idea of refurbishing it for use as his summer home, but when renovation costs started to creep above the $50 million mark, he decided to turn it into a boutique hotel – possibly the most glamorous boutique hotel in the world. The thing that makes Villa Feltrinelli so special is that it has been kept entirely as a villa, providing an extraordinary opportunity to experience a genuine Belle Epoque palace exactly as it was intended. The bedrooms are the original bedrooms; the same goes for the *Gone with the Wind* marble staircase, the entrance foyer, the living rooms, the dining room, the library... Nothing has been changed architecturally. Unlike other palaces that have been divided into shoeboxes, at Feltrinelli you are more like a house guest in a villa. Villa Feltrinelli is the embodiment of a bygone era of luxury and sophistication – the chance to live like a doge for the day...or longer, if the budget allows.

Here's an extraordinary adventure that even the Feltrinellis may not have thought of. Villa Feltrinelli has a shiny mahogany boat, and the most unforgettable way to make use of it is to get dressed up in black tie and evening dress, sashay down the marble staircase, amble onto the Venetian dock and take the boat south – just in time to catch the opera at Verona's famous outdoor Roman Arena. Afterwards, the boat will take you back to your splendid Belle Epoque villa on the lake, gliding through inky dark waters while the on-board stewards serve you a late supper. You simply can't get better than that!

VENICE

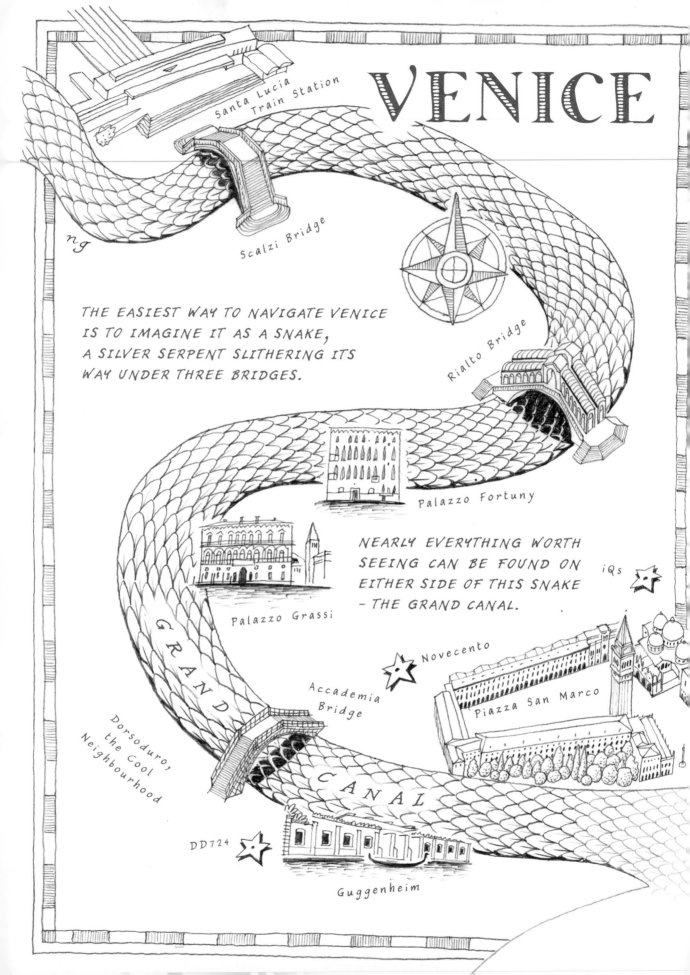

VENICE

Santa Lucia
Train Station

ng

Scalzi Bridge

Rialto Bridge

THE EASIEST WAY TO NAVIGATE VENICE
IS TO IMAGINE IT AS A SNAKE,
A SILVER SERPENT SLITHERING ITS
WAY UNDER THREE BRIDGES.

Palazzo Fortuny

NEARLY EVERYTHING WORTH
SEEING CAN BE FOUND ON
EITHER SIDE OF THIS SNAKE
– THE GRAND CANAL.

iQs

Palazzo Grassi

Novecento

GRAND

Accademia
Bridge

Piazza San Marco

Dorsoduro,
the Cool
Neighbourhood

CANAL

DD724

Guggenheim

The Most Exotic
City in the World

*When I went to Venice, I found that my dream had
become – incredibly, but quite simply – my address!*

Marcel Proust

Who doesn't dream of Venice? This has been the world's most exotic city for more
than a thousand years. With its maze of canals and its Gothic palaces and churches,
built on wooden stilts in the middle of a vast lagoon, Venice was, and still is, one of
the most extraordinary feats of engineering. If we are amazed by it today, imagine
the impression it must have made at a time when the rest of Europe was struggling
to emerge from the filth and darkness of the Middle Ages. Venice, in medieval times,
must have appeared like a vision from another world.

Not only was it, at the time, the largest city in Italy, but it was also the most
liberal and cosmopolitan place in Europe. Venice was busy trading with cultures
and corners of the world that people didn't even know existed, at a time when
few dared to venture out of their own village. And of course, when the most
famous Venetian merchant of them all, Marco Polo, returned from half a lifetime
in the Orient, in 1295, Venice also briefly held the distinction of being the first
city-state in Europe to establish a relationship with the most mysterious culture of
them all: China.

A lot has changed since 'Marco Milione' – as Polo was often called in jest, because
his stories seemed so far-fetched (as in, 'the Marco that told a million lies') – first got
back from Kublai Khan's empire, but Venice is still Venice – one of the most magical
places in the world.

JUMP
INTO A
UNIQUE
TAXI

Let's be very clear: in Venice, the taxi is Venice. Everything that is different and exciting and memorable about Venice is embodied in these slick, gleaming mahogany vessels that power so elegantly through this one-of-a-kind 'rococo waterworld'. Where else can you step off a plane straight onto a beautiful motorboat that can whisk you – via lagoon and canals – to the front door of your hotel or apartment?

Yes, it's true, you could also opt for the *vaporetto*, the Venice equivalent of a bus. It's a public transport option that also travels on the water, but that's missing the point. Venice water taxis are not just about being on the water. They are about style and grace and extravagance. When was the last time you heard those words used to describe a taxi? Venetian taxi drivers are obsessed with their streamlined speedboats. They wash them, they polish them, they varnish them, they pamper them; they take pride in keeping them in immaculate condition. Why? Because they are Venetian, and Venetians throughout history have been obsessed with the water around them, and with fine craftsmanship.

A Venetian water taxi turns an airport commute into a thirty-minute adventure. It offers a journey on waterways that have remained unchanged for hundreds of years – a cultural experience that substitutes for the usual and more mundane exercise of simply getting from 'A' to 'B'. In almost all other travel scenarios, the trip from the airport is something you'll probably want to forget. In Venice, it sets the tone; at least, it should do. The price is fixed (around 120 euros for the entire boat), so if you are with friends the cost per person goes down accordingly. But even if you are on your own, it is worth it for the simple reason that it is unique. Spending 120 euros on a memory you will never forget seems like money well spent.

CITIZEN OF VENICE

Heroic Busts of the Everyday Venetian

Italy has more than its fair share of monumental statues and busts. Both the Roman Empire and the Renaissance made significant contributions to a staggering portfolio. The quality of all this carved stone is impressive, to say the least, but the imagination involved in terms of subject matter? Not so much. The Romans stuck to a strict diet of Hercules and Caesar. The Renaissance was particularly fond of David. Heroes, emperors, mythical figures and biblical characters were the rule, and the rule was rarely broken. One of the only places in Italy – if not the only place – where you find heroic busts of the everyday citizen is in Venice. I love the idea that, hundreds of years ago, a soldier with a chubby face, sad eyes and a big helmet sat as a model for a skilled sculptor. It shows how enlightened and avant-garde the Venetians really were. At a time when almost all art was commissioned by cardinals and popes – in a bid to immortalize God – Venice was busy immortalizing the common man and woman.

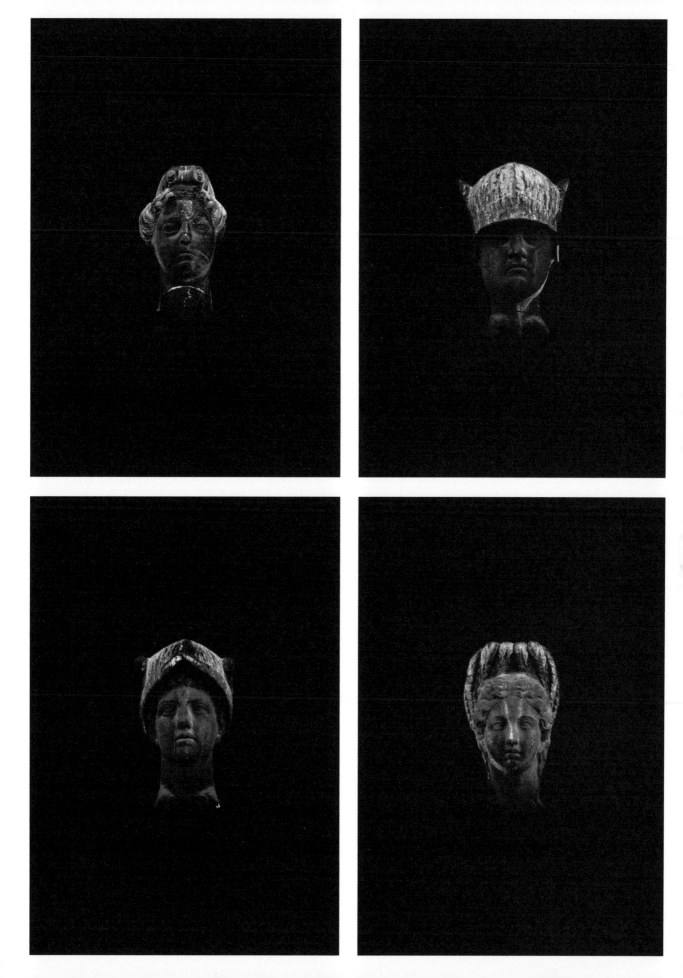

FORTUNY

The Enduring Legacy of a Creative Genius

Designer, photographer, collector, painter, inventor: Mariano Fortuny did it all. His former home, the Palazzo Fortuny in Campo San Beneto, was the Gothic forerunner to Andy Warhol's Factory. It was here that Fortuny invented the Moda Lamp, still a popular choice for contemporary interiors, the so-called Fortuny Dome (a system of indirect stage lighting for use in theatres), the Knossos scarf and, of course, the Grecian-inspired, figure-hugging Delphos silk gown – made using a cutting-edge pleating technique that he had developed and patented. The first wife of the influential Condé Nast had a purple one, and Peggy Guggenheim was frequently photographed wearing her gold one. More unusually, particularly considering the ruthless winds of change that blow through the fashion industry, a Delphos gown remains an object of desire more than a century after it was created.

All of Fortuny's creative pursuits – his lamps, his writings, his textile collection, his antique curios from ancient civilizations, his photographs, his own paintings (inspired by the work of Richard Wagner) and those of his father, his fabric designs, his drawings, his hand-painted velvets and silks, his patent applications – were scattered around his palazzo. The monumental spaces of the four-storey mansion functioned as a loft – possibly the most bohemian loft in Europe, and certainly the most exotic.

Fortuny died in 1949 but his widow, Henriette Nigrin, ensured the survival of his legacy by donating Palazzo Fortuny, along with most of its contents, to the city of Venice in 1965. Since then, it has operated as a museum. Because much of Fortuny's work is still in production, in-store and in demand, Palazzo Fortuny has a vibrancy and relevance that make it much more than a museum. It's fascinating to visit Fortuny's loft, which offers such insight into the manner of his creativity, and then to wander into a Venetia Studium boutique, where his dresses, lamps, velvets and silks are sold. It is all distinctly Venetian and decidedly oriental, yet it could have been created yesterday – and just like that, a hundred years disappear. As Oscar Wilde famously put it, 'All beautiful things belong to the same age.'

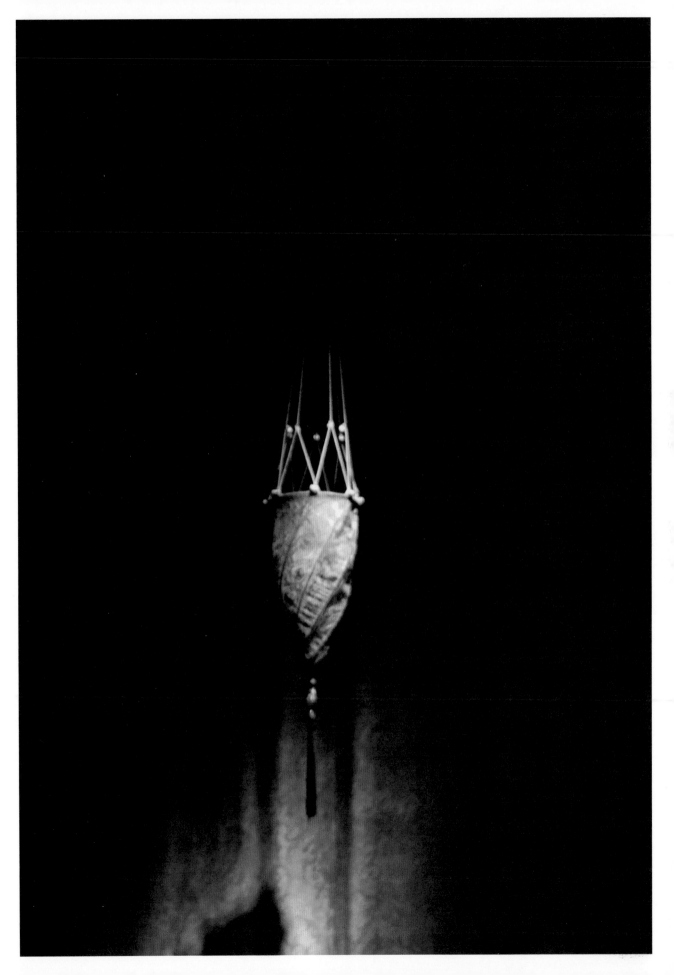

NOVECENTO

Inspired by Fortuny

Like most visitors to Venice, I am always looking for the authentic and the inspiring, but also for the new and the undiscovered. I think it's important for each new generation of traveller to put their own stamp on a destination, to reinvent priorities and find new places. That's why I was excited to discover Novecento, the first and only hotel in Venice to have been inspired, in decor, by Mariano Fortuny. The interior, certainly, could easily have been designed by him. There's an orientalist element at play that is both evocatively exotic and contemporary, but also quite appropriate to the city's heritage. At a time when most hotels in Venice offer cheap, unconvincing versions of 18th-century interiors and second-rate imitations of antiques, Novecento is clear, purposeful and relevant.

The beautiful rooms feature rugs from Morocco, cushions from Turkey, prayer beads from Thailand, pearl inlay from Damascus, and raw linens painted with oriental calligraphy, reflecting not just the tastes of Fortuny but also the legacy of trade with the Orient that built this city in the first place. For centuries, Venice was the most exotic city in the world. Venetian traders dared to venture further than any other merchants; to countries people had never heard of, to lands that were supposedly shut off from foreigners, such as China. They returned with items so exotic, so rare, that no one knew what to make of them. Marco Polo was the first and the most famous to venture into the forbidden empire, yet no one believed him when he returned to Venice a quarter of a century after he had left. Even this was typical of Venice: it has always been the city of theatrical illusion and fantasy, and Novecento taps into this without being clichéd or predictable.

It's typical of the approach of the Romanellis. This third-generation family of hoteliers strive to provide their guests with authenticity and charm without demanding the kind of prices that make other authentic addresses in Venice completely unattainable.

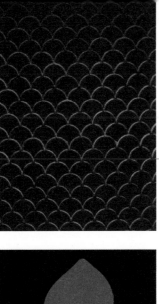

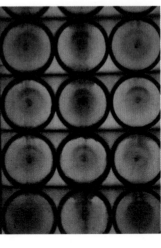

HOW MODERN ART SAVED VENICE

By the early part of the 20th century, Venice was in trouble. It was no longer powerful or rich. The trade that had once made this city flourish had long been forfeited to the world of international shipping. Trade between countries, and between continents, was now dominated by ports with little charm but plenty of technological infrastructure, such as Rotterdam and Hong Kong; ports designed purely for the loading and unloading of big ships.

Even the location of Venice, surrounded by water that had once protected it so well, was no longer relevant, at least not from a safety point of view. Now, the water, with the continual threat of flooding and a foul stench in the summer, seemed more of a burden than an asset. And the city's once scandalously liberal views were slowly being superseded by conservative attitudes, borne from fear of change and nostalgia for the glory days. Venice, in more ways than one, was sinking.

Luckily for Venice, just as it was losing its raison d'être, artists from all over the world started flocking to the city in droves. Painters, writers, photographers and filmmakers could not help but be swept up by the most imaginatively contrived city in the world. They didn't see loss of trade or dwindling wealth; they saw only the unique architecture – splendid palazzi with shiny terrazzo flooring, aristocratically

high ceilings and brilliant glass chandeliers – and the labyrinth of waterways dotted with black gondolas that had changed little in hundreds of years. It was all so much more than they could have imagined, and so they visited repeatedly and stayed as long as they could – some, permanently.

Writers such as Ernest Hemingway, Graham Greene and John Dos Passos were regulars at the Gritti Palace Hotel. Thomas Mann stayed at the Grand Hôtel des Bains on the Lido in 1911, which famously became the setting for his novella *Death in Venice*, published the following year; and Hemingway wrote about his host city in *Across the River and Into the Trees*, published in 1950, describing the hotels and the bars of Venice from the point of view of an American army colonel reminiscing about his times with Renata, a young Italian Contessa he had encountered during his tour of duty. The romantic notion of these famous writers, camped out in this extraordinary city, no doubt led to Venice's fledgling Film Festival also attracting greater numbers and more celebrated directors, including Frank Capra, Josef von Sternberg and John Ford by the 1930s.

But the individual who did most to secure the future of Venice was Peggy Guggenheim. By the time she arrived in 1948, Peggy – a member of the wealthy New York-based Guggenheim

dynasty (although not as wealthy as people may have imagined) – had long since established her credentials in the emerging world of modern art with her growing collection of works by artists such as Calder, Ernst, Man Ray, Miró, Magritte, Dalí, Klee, Chagall, Arp, Braque, Kandinsky, Brancusi, Moore, Duchamp, Picasso and Pollock; and she had started to cement her reputation as a visionary, buying works from artists who were unknown at the time but who would go on to become household names. Her career began with a gallery in London, but Venice would prove to be much more her cup of tea. The opportunity to purchase the famously unfinished Palazzo Venier dei Leoni on the Grand Canal, next to the Accademia Bridge, gave her the high-profile foothold she needed. The single-storey building (only the ground floor was ever completed) was perfect for her because it appeared, despite its 18th-century vintage, convincingly modern, and the long flat roof gave her somewhere to entertain and sunbathe. Once she moved in, she never left.

Peggy Guggenheim was more than a passionate collector. She lived, breathed and slept art. The artists she collected were her friends, her lovers and her society. She was shrewd in her judgment and purchased works at a time when the artists had little or no currency. Needless to say, their profiles were attached to hers and as she became more famous and respected, and an invitation to her unique art-filled abode on the Grand Canal became increasingly sought after, their prices started to rise in step with her ascending influence and power. Eventually, her collection would prove to be priceless.

Peggy brought to Venice what the city badly needed: a new and vibrant direction, and the opportunity to reinvent itself. Modern art was the perfect fit. The presence of these modern artists in this old city provided a catalyst, not only for the emerging world of tourism but also for the many artisan disciplines the city had cultivated, and dominated, over the centuries. Glassblowers in Murano, inspired by the likes of Calder, Miró and Picasso, stopped making copies of baroque chandeliers and fussy rococo wine glasses and started producing stunningly modern glassware that featured imaginative swirls of extraordinarily bright colours. Modern Murano glass captured the world's attention with works by studio names such as Venini, and it became highly sought after and collectable. Today, these pieces are sold as valuable works of art in their own right, not just in the chichi galleries of Venice but all over the world.

Guggenheim's modern art invasion also inspired local design. Acclaimed architect Carlo Scarpa garnered worldwide fame for his minimal but ethereal designs, drawing on Venetian influences and materials, such as mosaics, marble, glass and gold leaf, to create a new aesthetic. Mariano Fortuny, too, benefited from Peggy's patronage.

All of it – the art, the authors, the revitalized artisan traditions, the re-edit of Venetian ingredients in modern design, the film festival – kickstarted something deep and meaningful and lasting for Venice: an identity with art that continues to this day. Venice is once again influential in the world of the arts, just as it was in the past. The Biennale is the most prestigious and important art event in the world, and since 2006 Palazzo Grassi, an imposing palace on the Grand Canal, has been home to the French billionaire François Pinault's formidable collection of modern art – even though every city in France would have given their right arm to build a museum for it.

Peggy Guggenheim died in 1979 but her splendid palazzo and much of her collection survive today as a museum of modern art – the Peggy Guggenheim Collection – which, rightfully, has become one of the most visited attractions in Venice. Even today, more than seven decades after she first arrived in Venice, her juxtaposition of vibrant and colourful modern art with the city's historic opulence remains powerful, inspiring and thoroughly contemporary.

COCKTAILS ON THE GRAND CANAL

Thinking about dropping into Harry's Bar, before dinner, for a few of their famous Bellinis (Giuseppe Cipriani's invention)? So are 5,000 other people. If you like queuing, please do! Yes, it's true, Hemingway and other countless legends used to come here, but they didn't have to wait their turn. To be frank: the heyday of Harry's Bar is long gone. That's life! Things change! Venice is a city, not a museum, and like all cities there's a flux and flow to the restaurant and bar scene. There are other places for cocktails...

Like the bar at Palazzina G, on Ramo Grassi, with its glass wall that faces directly on to the Grand Canal. It's surreal to sit at the bar, under Philippe Starck's melting chandeliers, watching water taxis and other craft racing past you or even straight at you. It turns the Grand Canal into a movie. The atmosphere is like a gentlemen's 'members-only' club – a club that caught

fire and melted. I love the sense of humour to it. It is vintage Starck.

Starck has plenty of history with Venice. He was using Venetian mirrors in his design projects (such as the Royalton in New York and the Delano in Miami) long before most people even knew what Venetian mirrors were. He became such a champion of the Venetian mirror that he acquired a small house on the island of Burano so that he could spend more time with the craftsmen doing his bidding.

But back to Harry's Bar... You can't *not* go to Harry's Bar – your grandmother back home will never forgive you because that's what she did. I understand! It's a bonding thing. If you must go, take my advice and opt for an early lunch. You can still have your Bellini, the food is good, and the crowds won't be arriving until later. Even the waiters might be civil. Maybe.

DD724

Channelling Peggy

Down a little side street off Calle della Chiesa, a few doors from the canal that runs along the back of the Peggy Guggenheim Collection, is an unobtrusive house called DD724. The letters 'DD' are a reference to Dorsoduro, a trendy area of Venice filled with boutiques, bars, restaurants and galleries. This was Peggy Guggenheim's neighbourhood, and it shows. Some galleries – no bigger than a closet – feature exquisite examples of modern Murano glass by legends such as Carlo Scarpa, and there are small trattorias by lesser-known canals that experience none of the heavy footfall that can overwhelm other parts of Venice.

Although you could never tell from the outside, DD724 – set within the framework of an old Venetian house, with rugged beams and uneven walls that have sagged over the years – is filled with modern art. The entrance features an installation of black silk butterflies swarming over the walls and staircase in monumental numbers, and the emphasis on modern art continues through to the dining room, the library and the guest rooms. There's a tangible vibrancy and energy to DD724. The neighbourhood is young, the attitude is young, and the art is young – providing the perfect contrast with Venice, which is so wonderfully old.

CHARMING HOUSE IQS

A Venetian Boathouse Doubles as a Memorable Living Room

Dorsoduro is not the only quiet, less touristy neighbourhood in Venice. On the other side of the city, a brisk twenty-minute walk from the Accademia Bridge, is an area known as Querini Stampalia (hence the 'Q' and the 'S'). It is defined by a beautiful square, called Campo Santa Maria Formosa, built around the imposing façade of a Renaissance church of the same name.

Just around the corner, hidden by the bulk of the church, is a 15th-century palazzo called Casa Venier. It was the birthplace of the celebrated admiral Sebastiano Venier, who was Doge of Venice from 1577 to 1578. The entrance can only be reached by way of its own private footbridge across a small canal. The massive wooden door on the other side of the bridge leads straight into an internal courtyard that has not changed much in the past 600 years. There's a circular stone well in the centre, and an overhanging 15th-century wooden balcony suspended from the first floor creates a corridor that hides several doorways leading to different residential apartments. One of these is the entrance to iQs.

Upon opening the door, you immediately jump forward six centuries. The modernity is a startling surprise, a profound but successful contrast with the Gothic architecture. Perhaps not surprisingly, this complex of three uncluttered modern apartments belongs to Chiara Bocchini, who also owns DD724. She has a distinct signature – a stylish sense of how to blend antique and modern successfully. This was a building she already knew well because she lives upstairs.

A quick word about the apartments: in a city where everyone adjusts their expectations – anticipating small rooms and perhaps little style – iQs bucks the trend. These apartments, by Venetian standards, by any standards, are huge, plus you get the added benefit that they are, as the French say, *pieds dans l'eau*. The water of two canals laps up against the walls, just under your windows. Rio de Santa Maria Formosa runs under the private bridge, and Rio del Mondo Novo runs past the boathouse of the palazzo.

The boathouse, by the way, is definitely the most special feature of iQs. The water from the canal runs right into the house, up to a stone staircase that is partially submerged, or not, depending on the tide. There's also a dock, a catwalk of sorts that folds out in case you choose to arrive by water taxi or gondola. But the part that is most captivating is that the boathouse has been reinvented as a living room, complete with coffee-making apparatus, couches, magazines and music. It quickly became my favourite place to be. I loved watching gondolas float past and the stunned faces of tourists as they spotted me, coffee in hand, looking back at them.

CARLO SCARPA

Master of Modern Design

Carlo Scarpa was a 20th-century Venetian architect, designer and professor who famously took inspiration from his birthplace and used materials that were historically associated with the city, such as bronze, glass, travertine, gold leaf, iron, stone, mosaic tiles and terrazzo, in new, highly inventive ways. No one was more skilled at mixing these elements together, which is why he was sometimes called 'the alchemist'.

Often, he would use the entire repertoire in one venue. A wonderful example is the showroom he designed for Olivetti on Piazza San Marco. It's hard to imagine now, but the typewriter was the smartphone of the 1950s, and the most stylish and sought-after typewriters were by Olivetti. Asking Scarpa to design their showroom was the same as Apple, today, asking Norman Foster to design their new circular campus in Silicon Valley. For Olivetti, Scarpa pulled out all the stops: rough-edged marble mosaics in different colours, polished terrazzo, moulded concrete, polished cement, angle iron, wooden joinery, bronze detailing, all mixed together in a minimal but strangely exotic way. Even the sign outside was crafted from a rough-hewn block of marble with only the Olivetti letters cut and polished, like typewriter keys. It was an exaggerated mix but, like a complex recipe in the hands of a master chef, it worked.

The typewriter has had its day, but the showroom, which is still exactly as Scarpa designed it, has become one of the most fascinating (and lesser-known) venues to visit in Venice. It is a testament not only to Scarpa, but also to the longevity of the ingredients of the Venetian style.

A DAY AT
THE BEACH
IN VENICE

Look at archived glamour photos of 1950s movie stars and you will probably find pictures of them frolicking on the beach in Venice. Yes, Venice, Italy. This is certainly true of Kirk Douglas, seen on the sand flexing his *Spartacus* muscles for Brigitte Bardot before heading out into the Adriatic to show off his water skills. Or Paul Newman, sporting a beard and short shorts, emerging from the sea and gracefully accommodating the eager paparazzi.

Nowadays few people even know Venice has a beach, and yet – especially in summer – it could, and should, be part of your Venice adventure. It's a welcome respite from the crowds and the heat, and it's surprisingly easy to achieve: all you need is a water taxi. Just mention one word – 'Lido' – to the driver and he will do the rest. It's no more than fifteen minutes across the lagoon, and from the pier where the taxi drops you off it's a five-minute walk to the beach. It's certainly not what you might think. The beach is huge, a broad stretch of pale sand that goes on uninterrupted for many kilometres. Better

still, the only people on it are holidaying Italians, and not that many, even in peak season. Behind the beach, this island that looks back at Venice sitting in its lagoon is shaded by mature plane trees, and the noise from the cicadas chirping away is strangely welcome and reassuring. This is a completely different world from touristy Venice, and the best way to explore it is to hire a bicycle. With a bike you can get around and discover the little bakeries, trattorias and pizza places hidden away on this lush, low-key island. You will also likely stumble across the very white and very modern architectural complex called the Palazzo del Cinema, purpose-built in 1937 for the Venice Film Festival, the world's oldest film festival. And no doubt you will cycle past the historic Hotel Excelsior on the beach – the scene of many a celebrity reception.

You could even 'reverse-engineer' your Venice experience. Why not stay in a beautiful (and much cheaper) hotel on the Lido, on or near the beach, and make your way to Venice by water taxi whenever you want?

VENISSA

Rare Wine in a Unique Setting

It's easy to forget that Venice is not the only island in the lagoon. There are many others – some well known, such as Murano, and others that are virtually unheard of. I'm sure most Venetians would have trouble reciting the names of all the isles that lie in this vast expanse of sheltered water. Yet it hasn't always been this way.

Centuries ago, the population was more evenly spread across the various islands in the lagoon. That's why you will find impressively large churches on islands with only a few inhabitants; imposing places of worship built at a time when these tiny specks hosted sizeable towns.

Mazzorbo is exactly such an island. All that is left from a previous period of prosperity is the bell tower of what must have once been an important church. The land where the chapel used to stand is now a small vineyard that produces some 4,000 bottles of wine a year.

It is a very special wine, and not just because it is produced in such limited quantities: it is made from a grape that was thought to be extinct. The Dorona is the stuff of legend, a golden-coloured grape – unique to the Venetian Lagoon, from the time of the doges – that was considered unparalleled in its sweetness and crisp palate. Sadly, it had long since ceased to exist – at least, that's what everyone thought. But then it was discovered, growing on a potted vine in a convent, on a nearby island. It was an extraordinary find and it raised the question of whether there might be more surviving examples out there – which there were.

Eventually, by pooling all these newly discovered vines and grafting them, there were enough to plant a tiny vineyard. With the first harvest in 2010, it seemed only fitting that the bottles were hand-blown on Murano by Giovanni Moretti; he suggested that the artisan Mario Berta Battiloro, from a family known for making gold leaf, produce a sheet of gold leaf as a label, which Moretti then fired into the glass. No branding, no predictable line drawing depicting the vineyard: just a subtle and refined object of beauty that happens to blend two Venetian traditions.

The wine and the winery were only the beginning. Venissa is also a small boutique hotel and restaurant. The restaurant, not surprisingly given the admirable way they approach things here, has earned a Michelin star, and the accommodation has proved so popular that they have added more rooms in the colourful houses of nearby Burano, an island linked by a wooden footbridge. This is more than a memorable place for lunch: it's an inspiring and authentic experience with a story to tell that just happens to include a bonus of delicious food and memorable wine – a reminder of the true and timeless culture of Venice.

CONTACTS

SICILY

Casa Talía
Via Exaudinos, 1/9
Modica
Tel: +39 0932 752075
www.casatalia.it

Hotel Gutkowski
Lungomare di Levante
Elio Vittorini, 26
96100 Syracuse
Tel: +39 0931 465861
www.guthotel.it

Monaci delle Terre Nere
Via Monaci
95019 Zafferana Etnea
Tel: +39 095 708 3638
www.monacidelleterrenere.it

Villa Ducale
Via Leonardo Da Vinci, 60
98039 Taormina
Tel: +39 0942 28153
www.villaducale.com

Masseria Susafa
Contrada Susafa – Polizzi Generosa
90028 Palermo
Tel: +39 091 7487477
www.susafa.com

Villa Romana del Casale
94015 Piazza Armerina
www.villaromanadelcasale.it

Castello di Falconara
Strada Statale 115, Km. 245
93011 Butera
Tel: +39 091 329 082
www.castellodifalconara.it

AEOLIAN ISLANDS

Hotel Signum – Salina
Via Scalo, 15
98050 Malfa
Tel: +39 090 984 42 22
www.hotelsignum.it

NAPLES

Hotel Excelsior
Via Partenope, 48
Lungomare Caracciolo
80121 Naples
Tel: +39 081 764 0111
www.eurostarshotels.co.uk

Ristorante Pizzeria Mattozzi
Via Gaetano Filangieri, 16
80121 Naples
Tel: +39 081 416378

Museo Archeologico Nazionale
di Napoli
Piazza Museo, 19
80135 Naples
www.museoarcheologiconapoli.it

Terrazza Calabritto
Piazza Vittoria, 1
80121 Naples
Tel: +39 081 240 5188
www.terrazzacalabritto.it

Casa di Anna
Via Sant'Anna dei Lombardi, 36
80100 Naples
http://acasadianna.eu

Casa D'Anna
Via dei Cristallini, 138
80137 Naples
casadanna.it

AMALFI COAST

Parco dei Principi
Via Rota, 44
80067 Sorrento
Tel: +39 081 8782858
www.royalgroup.it/parcodeiprincipi

La Minervetta
Via Capo, 25
80067 Sorrento
Tel: +39 081 8774455
www.laminervetta.com

Villa Cimbrone
Via S. Chiara, 26
84010 Ravello
Tel: +39 089 857459
www.hotelvillacimbrone.com

Le Sirenuse
Via Cristoforo Colombo, 30
84017 Positano
Tel: +39 089 875066
www.sirenuse.it

CAPRI

Villa Jovis
Via Tiberio
80073 Capri

La Fontelina
Località Faraglioni
80073 Capri
Tel: +39 081 8370845
www.fontelina-capri.com

Punta Tragara
Via Tragara, 57
80073 Capri
Tel: +39 081 8370844
www.hoteltragara.com

MATERA

Le Grotte della Civita
Via Civita, 28
(Sasso Barisano)
75100 Matera
Tel: +39 0835 332744
legrottedellacivita.sextantio.it

PUGLIA

Masseria Alchimia
Contrada Fascianello, 50
72015 Fasano
Tel: +39 335 609 46 47
www.masseria-alchimia.it

Masseria Prosperi
S.P. 366, Km. 23 –
Località Frassanito
73028 Otranto – Lecce
Tel: +39 333 1360671
masseriaprosperi.it

Convento di Santa Maria di
Costantinopoli
Via Convento
Marittima di Diso
mcalpine@convento.co.uk

Ristorante Lo Scalo
Marina di Novaglie
73034 Lecce
Tel: +39 0833 533488
www.ristoranteloscalo.it

ROME AND LAZIO

Le Jardin de Russie
Via del Babuino, 9
00187 Rome
Tel: +39 06 32888870
www.roccofortehotels.com

Ristorante Atelier Canova Tadolini
Via del Babuino, 150a
00187 Rome
Tel: +39 06 32110702
www.canovatadolini.com

Hotel Locarno
Via della Penna, 22
00186 Rome
Tel: +39 06 3610841
www.hotellocarno.com

Quinto
Via di Tor Millina, 15
00186 Rome
Tel: +39 06 6865657
www.quintogel.it

Trattoria al Moro
Vicolo delle Bollette, 13
00187 Rome
Tel: +39 06 6783495
www.ristorantealmororoma.com

Corte della Maestà
Via della Provvidenza
01022 Civita di Bagnoregio
Tel: +39 335 8793077
www.cortedellamaesta.com

La Posta Vecchia
Palo Laziale
00055 Palo Laziale
Tel: +39 06 9949501
www.postavecchiahotel.com

UMBRIA

Eremito
Località Tarina 2
05010 Parrano (Terni)
Tel: +39 0763 891010
www.eremito.com

Borgo di Carpiano
Località Carpiano
06024 Gubbio
Tel: +39 075 920337
www.borgodicarpiano.com

SARDINIA

L'Agnata di De André
Località L'Agnata
07029 Tempio Pausania
Tel: +39 079 671384
www.agnata.com

Faro Capo-Spartivento
Viale Spartivento
09010 Domus de Maria
Tel: +39 393 8276800
www.farocapospartivento.com

FLORENCE AND TUSCANY

Il Borro Tuscan Bistro
Lungarno degli Acciaiuoli, 80r
50100 Florence
Tel: +39 055 290423
www.ilborrotuscanbistro.it

Hotel Savoy
Piazza della Repubblica, 7
50123 Florence
Tel: +39 055 27351
www.roccofortehotels.com

La Terrazza, Hotel Continentale
Vicolo dell'Oro, 6r
50123 Florence
Tel: +39 055 2762 4000
www.lungarnocollection.com

Riva Lofts
Via Baccio Bandinelli, 98
50142 Florence
Tel: +39 055 7130272
www.rivalofts.com

SoprArno Suites
Via Maggio, 35
50125 Florence
Tel: +39 055 0468718
www.soprarnosuites.com

Borgo Santo Pietro
Località Palazzetto
53012 Chiusdino
Tel: +39 0577 751222
www.borgosantopietro.com

Castello di Vicarello
58044 Poggi del Sasso
Cinigiano
Tel: +39 0564 990718
castellodivicarello.com

MILAN

Bulgari Hotel
Via Privata Fratelli Gabba, 7b
20121 Milan
Tel: +39 02 805 805 1
www.bulgarihotels.com

Il Salumaio di Montenapoleone
Palazzo Bagatti Valsecchi
Via S. Spirito, 10 / Via Gesù, 5
Tel: +39 02 76001123
www.ilsalumaiodimontenapoleone.it

Grand Hotel Tremezzo
Via Regina, 8
22016 Tremezzo
Tel: +39 0344 42491
www.grandhoteltremezzo.com

VERONA AND
LAKE GARDA

The Gentleman of Verona
Via Carlo Cattaneo, 26/a
37121 Verona
Tel: +39 045 8009566
www.thegentlemanofverona.com

Villa Feltrinelli
Via Rimembranza, 38–40
25084 Gargnano
Tel: +39 0365 79 80 00
www.villafeltrinelli.com

VENICE

Palazzo Fortuny
San Marco 3958
30124 Venice
Tel: +39 041 5200995
fortuny.visitmuve.it

Novecento
San Marco 2683/84
30124 Venice
Tel: +39 041 2413765
www.novecento.biz

Peggy Guggenheim Collection
Palazzo Venier dei Leoni
Dorsoduro 701
30123 Venice
Tel: +39 041 2405 411
www.guggenheim-venice.it

Palazzina G
Ramo Grassi
Sestiere San Marco 3247
30124 Venice
Tel: +39 041 5284644
www.palazzinag.com

DD724
Dorsoduro 724
30123 Venice
Tel: +39 041 2770262
www.thecharminghouse.com

Charming House iQs
Campiello Querini Stampalia
Castello 4425
30122 Venice
Tel: +39 041 2410062
www.thecharminghouse.com

Negozio Olivetti
Piazza San Marco 101
30124 Venice
Tel: +39 041 5228387
www.negoziolivetti.it
www.fondoambiente.it

Venissa
Fondamenta S. Caterina, 3
30142 Mazzorbo
Tel: +39 041 52 72 281
www.venissa.it

INDEX

New Map Italy © 2019 Thames & Hudson Ltd, London

New Map™ is a trademark of Herbert Ypma. All Rights Reserved.

Text © 2019 Herbert Ypma
Photographs © 2019 Herbert Ypma
Photograph on p. 345 © Photo Awakening/Getty Images
Hand-drawn maps and illustrations (including cover) © 2019 Neil Gower

Layout by Herbert Ypma
Art direction by Linda Lundin

First published in 2019 in the United States of America by
Thames & Hudson Inc., 500 Fifth Avenue, New York, New York 10110

www.thamesandhudsonusa.com

Library of Congress Control Number 2018946279

ISBN 978-0-500-29288-4

Printed and bound in China by C&C Offset Printing Co. Ltd